*Listen to your small whisper and make it grow into a dream. — Pa Roamu*

# Giving The Ultimate Gift

*You are the Ultimate Gift!*

*♡ Amy McDam*

Published by Game Changer Publishing

Paperback ISBN: 978-1-963793-21-5
Hardcover ISBN: 978-1-963793-22-2
Digital: ISBN: 978-1-963793-23-9

www.GameChangerPublishing.com

TO:

_____

FROM:

_____

DATE:

_____

# DEDICATION

*"This book is dedicated to my late, great mother, Florene Stovall, who taught me the principles that I shared with the world in The Ultimate Gift book and movie. It is also dedicated to the thousands of mothers who shared the messages in The Ultimate Gift with their sons, creating a tidal wave of giving, learning, and growing that is changing our world."*

   – Jim Stovall

*"I would like to dedicate this book to my mom, Margaret Stiles. She always encouraged me to be strong, work hard, and modeled that women can do and be whatever they set their sights on. She was my biggest cheerleader in the development of Young Men's Service League, and she loved that we strived to lead young men in such a positive way. I also want to honor the hundreds of women on our leadership team who have traveled this journey with me. Their passion, gifts, and talents have made YMSL a wonderful organization with a tremendous culture of supporting and growing while filled with grace for others. Last but not least, thank you to my family, who have sacrificed and supported me all along the way."*

   – Pam Rosener

# Read This First

Just to say thanks for buying and reading our book, we would like to give you a few free bonus gifts, no strings attached!

**To Download Your Free Gifts, Scan the QR Code:**

# Giving The Ultimate Gift

*Transforming Communities & Cultivating Compassion:*

*A Look at the Young Men's Service League*

**Jim Stovall and Pam Rosener**

www.GameChangerPublishing.com

# Author's Welcome

My Dear Reader,

I want to thank you for the investment of time and money you have made in taking this journey with me within the pages of this book. For some readers, this will be our first journey together, while others have traveled with me many times throughout my more than 50 books and the nine movies based on my novels. Among all of my titles, this book is unique as it exists to share the impact that one of my other books, and the movie based upon it, has had in the real world with real people.

As a blind person myself, I remember spending an entire afternoon at the Louvre Museum in Paris, sitting outside the gallery where Leonardo da Vinci's legendary painting, the Mona Lisa, was displayed. Obviously, without my sight, I was not able to appreciate Leonardo's work firsthand, but I got to experience the Mona Lisa through the eyes, the passion, and the awe of people from all around the world who saw that masterpiece.

Many readers of this book may have read *The Ultimate Gift* or seen the movie based on it, while others have not. I was a reluctant and somewhat unintentional author. Being visually impaired, I never intended to be a reader, let alone a writer. My success as an athlete, becoming a national Olympic weightlifting champion, and my business success in creating the Narrative Television Network—which culminated in an Emmy Award—brought me into the spotlight as a corporate speaker and created demand for a book. My first five books were success-oriented, non-fiction business titles. They were very well received in the marketplace, but when my publisher demanded still another book, I realized I had written everything I knew and a few things I merely suspected, so it was time for me to consider writing fiction.

*The Ultimate Gift* was my first foray into the world of writing novels. I wrote the book in five inspired, frantic days in my office between my meetings and phone calls. I would describe it as a subconscious creation or a divine download. I merely dictated the book as it flowed through me and literally never read it until years later when esteemed actor Tom Bosley of *Happy Days* and *Father Dowling* fame recorded the audio version of *The Ultimate Gift*. When I listened to that audiobook in its entirety on a long flight, I was struck by the fact that there were great portions of the story I couldn't even remember. I experienced the story of *The Ultimate Gift* much as millions of readers and movie audiences have around the world throughout the years.

That original *Ultimate Gift* novel has spawned three sequel books and a movie trilogy that has become somewhat of a worldwide phenomenon. The story of *The Ultimate Gift* centers around an iconic self-made billionaire named Red Stevens. As an oil and cattle baron, he conquered the world of business but totally neglected his family. Late in his life, he realized the disaster that would occur if he passed on his immense accumulation of valuables without also passing along the values he learned through creating business success. Red felt that his grandson, Jason Stevens, was the one person in the family who had a spark of hope and a bit of raw potential and promise. Instead of making Jason an instant billionaire through his will, Red designed a twelve-month odyssey that would take Jason through monthly quests that would lead to the ultimate gift.

Jason had been a spoiled, entitled young man throughout his life, so being exposed to the gift of work, the gift of problems, the gift of gratitude, and all of the other lessons was quite alien to him. Only when he could prove to Red Stevens' lifelong friend and attorney, Mr. Hamilton, that he had grasped each of the concepts and overcome every hurdle, could Jason obtain the ultimate gift and his inheritance. I won't spoil the climax of that book and movie, but within these pages, you will experience *The Ultimate Gift* through the mothers and sons in the Young Men's Service League.

Within these pages, you are going to relive how *The Ultimate Gift* impacted some mothers who shared it with their sons who then breathed life into that message and brought it to those in need—much as I experienced the Mona Lisa through the impact it had on those who saw it firsthand.

The credit and accolades for this movement of service and generosity should be directed toward the mothers and sons who made it happen. *The Ultimate Gift* was nothing more than an idea in my head or words on a page until the special people involved in the Young Men's Service League brought the book and movie to life through the thousands of Ultimate Gift service projects they carried out during their high school years.

As you read these young men's stories in their own words, I hope you will be both inspired and challenged, but beyond that, I hope you will be moved to the extent that you will begin thinking about how you can bring *The Ultimate Gift* to life in the world around you.

– Jim Stovall

# Praise from Ultimate Gift Service Project Recipients

"...To know there will be people who will come out on a Saturday or Sunday because you care. We want them (our clients) to feel seen, like they belong, and are important. They matter. They are not alone. You are not volunteers when you come in for these projects. You are not volunteers. You are serving and loving people through your actions by showing up as a complete stranger... Nobody does this. But you do it, and I am proud of this organization."

**Ken Carpenter, Jubilee Reach**

"You all brought so much to HopeFest and made this our best year ever... ...by my rough count, I have attendance at approximately 4,200 people, which is our record. Even more important was the quality of so much of the day. The bike rodeo, field games, craft area, children's clothing, etc., were all outstanding! Set up on Friday night was the smoothest we've ever had (even with the HUGE amount of clothing). And everyone, both moms and sons, were unfailingly positive and hard-working."

**Allen Weeks, Executive Director of**
**Austin Voices for Education and Youth**

"Last weekend, we had the pleasure of hosting over 200 YMSL volunteers between BBHH and our Learning Garden. Our Learning Garden was chosen as the Park Cities YMSL Chapter Ultimate Gift Site. Across Saturday and Sunday, volunteers worked tirelessly building and staining picnic tables and benches, planting bushes, building garden beds, and filling them with soil. We are SO grateful for all the hard work completed and all the donors who gave us *tools, beds, and donations to help make this possible. We are so excited for students at the school to learn and be hands-on in this new space. Thank you again to the Park Cities YMSL Chapter for making this dream a reality!"*

**Blane Rogers, Brother Bill's Helping Hand**
**(West Dallas STEM School Site Director)**

*"I want to thank you so much. Your organization has blessed us beyond measure with the gifts and toys we have here and the (Ultimate Gift) event in December. We could not have done it without YMSL. The word of mouth since that event has just been amazing. We now have 61 families on our respite care list, which is just amazing. The community is talking about our organization, and it's because of the event we had in December."*

**Lucy Wilson, Incredible Fridays Event Coordinator**

*"Thank you for collecting and assembling one thousand meal packs through your Ultimate Gift project. We are so grateful for your partnership in helping to fight food insecurity among kids in our community. We couldn't have done 1,000 meal packs on our own, so what you accomplished will greatly impact our community. We are so grateful."*

**Jennifer Lillis, Co-Founder of UP ministry**

*"Gateway was so excited to be the recipient of the YMSL Ultimate Gift. Helping us provide not only much-needed items but putting the effort into updating the center is truly a gift. The clothing closet has been completely reorganized and repurposed into an efficient and usable space. The women and children at Trinity were thrilled with their time at the zoo and the facelift their space received. (The women and children at Trinity Women's Shelter were treated to free admission to the Zoo, courtesy of Zoo Atlanta, while members and young men refreshed the common areas of their living space.) We appreciate YMSL's*

*support and assistance in assisting Atlanta's homeless population - it's unbelievable what this group accomplished in just one day!"*

**Drew Benton, Director of Community Engagement and Volunteer Services at Gateway Center Homeless Shelter**

*"...By pairing sons with their moms to experience AND MEET the needs of their community, young men begin at a young age to see the growing needs of our communities beyond the bubble in which they grow up. They learn that many families and children struggle daily to have a home, enough food, and health care. They learn the long-term oppressive and detrimental impact of poverty, abuse, and homelessness. Most importantly, they learn that their actions can help and begin to stop the cycle. The idea of social justice becomes real when they sit with, talk to, and personally help widows, orphans, and the least of these. For over 15 years, the young men and moms of the Young Men Service League have served alongside me in various ministries, serving in food pantries, repairing homes for homeless moms and children, mentoring young homeless children, and providing hope to women, children, families, and neighbors oppressed by the things of this world."*

**Rev. Janet Collinsworth, Agape Resource Center**

*"I wanted to tell you how much we appreciate all the volunteers and all the hard work that helped make the event successful. All of your volunteers were so nice and so willing to help even when we had to wait at times for instructions. I can't tell you how much we appreciated the help. We would have been there all night without your amazing folks."*

**Susan Baker, Operation Liberty Hill**

*"We truly and literally cannot thank you enough for the ALL that you did to make Ultimate Gift happen. Coordinating all of the many volunteers for*

manpower, getting all of the supplies, building the closets out, organizing all of the donations and supplies... It was A LOT of work, and it is so appreciated. We are so grateful. Last week, a mom of two of our students came in after school and asked us for clothing for her kids. They are staying in a shelter. As you can imagine, the way our donations were thrown into the closet, we were only able to dig through and give her a few things that were not even the right sizes. Now, BECAUSE OF YMSL, when this happens, we are able to invite our parents into our donation closet and allow them to pick out what they would like to have for their kids. It is incredible. We now know what we have and what we need so that we can properly serve our families. We could not have done it without you and without Young Men's Service League. Thank you for choosing to serve The Ansley School!"

**Becky Mautner, The Ansley School**

"We absolutely loved having the YMSL group. Everyone was very flexible and understanding of changes that popped up in the chaos of the holidays, and everyone was always on board to help out. It is such a blessing to have strong young men put in some muscle work for a female-dominated office! YMSL shows up to WORK! We could not have pulled off our Jingle Mingle event without y'all!! Everyone was on time and willing to do whatever we needed them to do and helped make our guests feel welcome. I cannot say THANK YOU enough."

**Brittany Jackson, Denton County Friends of the Family**

# Table of Content

# "The Inspiration"

*By Pam Rosener*

As Jim said in his welcome, you are about to embark on a journey of self-discovery of how the character in *The Ultimate Gift* is emulated in real life by the young men in YMSL Chapters across the United States. In their words, you get to read stories through the lens of young men who describe their experiences of giving, learning about the world around them, and realizing the impact of working together for the greater good. Our hope is that this not only inspires you but also renews hope for our future generations. The spirit of love beyond ourselves represented by these stories shows that our future as a nation will be bright when guided by the young men represented in this book.

Please read the Inspiration for a bit of background on the heart of YMSL and its journey to *Giving The Ultimate Gift*.

## Introduction to YMSL and Its Mission

In 2001, my sister-in-law Julie Rosener and I founded the Young Men's Service League (YMSL), a non-profit organization. YMSL's mission is threefold:

1. **Fostering Deeper Mother/Son Bonds:** YMSL is dedicated to enhancing the bonds between mothers and sons, nurturing stronger connections that enrich family relationships that then extend into

the broader community. Through this, we aim to cultivate values of empathy, compassion, and generosity for the ultimate benefit of society.

2. **Serving Our Communities:** YMSL is committed to positively impacting our communities. We achieve this by engaging in meaningful service projects that address diverse societal needs and challenges, support the less fortunate, and promote overall community well-being.

3. **Promoting Leadership Among Our Moms and Young Men:** We strive to build leadership qualities in our moms and our young men, equipping them to lead others. This empowerment benefits them personally and builds more robust, engaged communities and families.

YMSL was created in 2001 as an organization comprised of mothers and their high school-aged sons in grades 9 through 12. The founding leaders, including myself, set out with a primary goal: to foster stronger connections with our sons while serving those in need in our community. We not only wanted our sons to gain the importance of serving others, but we wanted to serve side by side with them. We wanted to be with them so we could see the "light bulb" go off and see their hearts grow. Since those early days, we have heard from thousands of moms that the most precious part of YMSL was the ride home after serving with their sons when mom and son bonded in new ways. They shared conversations about what part of their day touched them, about the hardships they now understood that others face and sometimes even just a laugh about something funny that happened. These moments are what we call the secret sauce of our organization. Most moms and sons will say that some of the best rides came after they did an Ultimate Gift project together.

YMSL also provides a comprehensive curriculum designed to equip our young men with essential life skills and leverage their innate strengths. This curriculum bridges their learning experiences at home, in school, at church, and through extracurricular activities. The meetings also provide our moms one more opportunity to connect with their sons as they share a conversation about a speaker or a class that taught them a new skill or revealed content that may help them make wiser decisions. These moments seem small but can have a tremendous impact over the four years of high school.

## Discovering *The Ultimate Gift*

At this point, you may be wondering how YMSL began its journey of "Giving the Ultimate Gift." It all began one day by chance. One of YMSL's philanthropic partners gifted me a copy of Jim's book. While the name of this generous person has been lost to time, I will never forget the impact this gift had on me and our organization. I devoured the book on the plane ride home from a YMSL trip. I was struck by the profound effect of the grandfather's wisdom and how he used a year to cultivate his grandson's mind and heart. When I finished reading the book and closed my eyes, I pondered how YMSL could apply these lessons to influence our young men similarly.

## The Correlation Between *The Ultimate Gift* and YMSL

Reflecting on the book's lessons and YMSL's goal of nurturing the minds and hearts of young men, we aim to ignite the spirit of giving and help them grasp the story's true meaning: "The only way you can truly get more out of life for yourself is to give part of yourself away."

Reading *The Ultimate Gift* ignited my desire to take YMSL from a focus on serving hours to those in need to what we could do that would have a larger impact in our communities. I immediately brainstormed ways to incorporate the book's lessons into our young men's curriculum and beyond. As a parent, I recognized my limitations and shortcomings in raising my children. I believed other moms would share similar feelings after reading the book, and I also wanted to provide them with a roadmap to help raise better young men.

I also realized that, while I had come to understand many of the gifts mentioned in the book, life experience had been my teacher. No one had imparted these principles to me during my teenage years. What if I had learned these lessons earlier? How could they have influenced my own life?

The book begins with the first gift—the gift of work. Many view work as a means to an end, but personally, I've always loved work and the sense of accomplishment that comes from a job well done. However, I recognized that not everyone shares this understanding, especially among our youth. For instance, in my own family, my kids have witnessed me performing various types of work. Take my love of gardening. My sons have questioned why I wouldn't simply pay someone else to garden for me.

Gardening exemplifies the gift of work perfectly. It starts with soil, planning a design, selecting plants, planting, nurturing them, and reaping the satisfaction of the beauty that work creates. I appreciate that the first chapter deals with work ethic—it's a perfect message for our young men. The work ethic of past generations is becoming lost, and the satisfaction of physical labor or a hard day's work is a vital part of growing to appreciate the simple things in life. *The Ultimate Gift* book offers many deeply impactful lessons, each special in its own way and collectively illustrating the true meaning of wealth in one's life. It is a priceless gift and captures many of the values we endorse in YMSL.

## Incorporating *The Ultimate Gift* into the YMSL Curriculum

To introduce the concepts from *The Ultimate Gift* to our YMSL moms and sons, we purchased multiple copies for each chapter and encouraged them to read the book. We even held a contest to see which chapter could engage the most moms and sons in reading the book. Additionally, we introduced the book's principles in our young men's meetings.

After reading the book, my vision extended beyond our organization. How could YMSL provide an Ultimate Gift to our communities? Could we create and implement a gift aligned with the book's initial gifts? Although we were a young organization then, we believed we could have a substantial impact if we united our efforts. So, we initiated the concept of the Ultimate

Gift Event and began exploring ways to make it a reality. This concept embodied the gift of Dreaming (mentioned in chapter 8 of *The Ultimate Gift*), emphasizing that dreamers need faith to envision the future.

## Growing Impact and Transition

In the early days of YMSL, I met extensively with the Executive Directors of our philanthropic partners to establish the relationships needed to provide the necessary service hours for our chapters. During these discussions, I learned about the significant unmet needs these organizations faced, and the idea that someone could tackle these needs left a strong impression on me. It reinforced my belief that we were on track to accomplish something remarkable in our community. While we were initially based in Plano, Texas, I envisioned our impact extending throughout the Dallas/Fort Worth metroplex and eventually across the nation.

In 2008, the City House of Plano, Texas, became the recipient of our first YMSL Ultimate Gift Event. City House provided shelter for teens, as homeless shelters typically did not cater to those aged fourteen to eighteen. Most local shelters require individuals to be adults for admission. At that time, we had approximately eight to ten chapters. We collaborated to complete a beautification project around the shelter's exterior, contributing over 500 hours of work across two weekends.

Due to their limited labor and funds resources, City House needed YMSL's help to achieve this. The project was a tremendous success, and it was inspiring to witness our moms and young men from multiple chapters working together to achieve a common goal. For many of our young men, this experience provided insight into the challenges faced by homeless teenagers who lack the love and support of a family. Understanding why the kids at City House had to live there made the young men's work more meaningful and heartfelt. They definitely went home that day realizing their blessings of having a home and a caring family.

## Expansion of Ultimate Gift Projects

Over the subsequent years, both YMSL and our Ultimate Gift Projects continued to grow. In 2010, we focused on the Douglas Community in Plano, Texas, an area rich in African-American history but facing economic hardships. Many homes were over seventy-five years old and in poor condition. Numerous elderly residents in the community could not maintain their homes and yards. Our project involved a range of tasks, from painting houses and removing trash to cleaning up yards and building fences. We also organized a "Dumpster" Day, where the young men collected trash and debris from neighborhood yards to fill dumpsters. The event allowed us to work alongside community members, creating meaningful connections. For example, we worked hand-in-hand with a differently-abled resident who volunteered to work alongside our crew to paint the exterior of his mom's home. The happiness she expressed at the end of the day by including her son and the beautification of her home was priceless and undoubtedly left a lasting memory for our volunteers.

In 2012, we conducted our last "National" Ultimate Gift. By then, we had nineteen Dallas/Fort Worth chapters. Over a few days, we completed twelve projects, from building a stage for an underprivileged school in Dallas to relocating a playground to a Section 8 housing development to a West Dallas neighborhood cleanup. It was an incredible collective effort, demonstrating the power of united action over a few weekends. That year, we realized that managing large-scale projects at a national level was becoming challenging, so we transitioned to having each chapter identify and manage its own projects going forward.

During that period, I worked closely with Karen Sharp, my co-chair for the event, who shared her thoughts with me in a letter.

*"My experience heading the Ultimate Gift Projects for YMSL National in the DFW metroplex holds such deep and wonderful memories, especially in the final year I chose to head up Ultimate Gifts. Organizing such a major one-*

*weekend volunteer effort for our chapters, which included project planning, funding, intense scheduling, ordering and delivering materials, logistics, and managing over 2,500 moms and sons volunteering their efforts and logging in their mom-son hours... WOW, what a FEAT that was!! Through it all, I learned so much more about the struggles of our metroplex, the needs of the people, and the many organizations and individuals who work thankless hours to help those in need. I wanted to show our sons that assisting folks is what you do. Watching the moms' efforts working in tandem with their sons was beautiful! It opened the eyes of our boys, which was a beautiful thing for them, as they took it all in while putting in the sweat and the time to help others less fortunate. We learned so much more about our fantastic city and its vast needs, while at the same time, we felt how much of a joy it was to make the time to help others. I will never forget this amazing experience! I thank YMSL for allowing me to further open my eyes and ears to this diverse world of needs and struggles and better understand how our boys, moms, and I can make a difference."*

—Karen Sharp

## Transitioning to Local Ultimate Gift Projects

For the next few years, local chapters began working to identify local Ultimate Gift Projects under the guidance of the national leadership team. At this point, our organization had 93 chapters, over half of which were doing an Ultimate Gift project in the fall/winter. That translated into over 500 moms and sons serving hundreds of hours together over 2-3 days to create change and give tremendously to each project within their community. Even with this amount of community impact, something still needed to be added to the service projects to incorporate the original lessons from Jim's book more closely. That something turned out to be a National Ultimate Gift Coordinator, Amy McDaniel.

Amy brought her enthusiasm from her chapter's Ultimate Gift project. She offered a fresh perspective on what these service events should represent.

Her process-driven approach breathed new life into the Ultimate Gift Projects. More importantly, her framework brought consistency to YMSL's approach now that each chapter was responsible for its own project.

She taught the twelve lessons from the book and fostered an "all in" mentality among chapter members and young men. Chapters began by identifying potential Ultimate Gift projects, conducting project selection, and then revealing the chosen project to the chapter. This reveal disclosed the beneficiary and emphasized the "WHO" they were serving.

Truthfully, this aspect was missing for years. Without an understanding of WHO and WHY they were serving, the impact of the service would be lost on the young men. This connection strengthened our Ultimate Gift program, deepening our ties with those we served and providing the young men with a transformative experience. Knowing the WHO put a face on the recipient, adding the human connection that etched the purpose of the gift into the heart.

Over the years, we've gained invaluable experiences. We've recently embarked on some significant projects in our larger cities that involve several chapters in multi-chapter events, with each chapter managing its own project with Amy's guidance.

## Future Goals and Impact

We are eager to see what opportunities lie ahead for YMSL. More and more philanthropic organizations nationwide are learning about our organization all the time. In fact, some are hearing about other philanthropies who have received an Ultimate Gift. We hope that one day, our program will become well-known enough that organizations in need will seek us out, making us a national resource for Ultimate Gifts.

During my life, it's been my practice to follow the small whispers in my quiet moments. Over fifteen years ago, I had one of those whispers after reading *The Ultimate Gift*. It urged me to challenge and change not only our young men but also our cities. ***In 2023, we served over 35,000+ hours on***

*Ultimate Gift projects.* I take immense joy in thinking about the number of lives transformed because I listened to that whisper of that dream.

The Ultimate Gift has become a cornerstone of the YMSL experience for our members and their sons during their four years with us. It allows us to instill something vital we could only accomplish with this foundation. We hope that as these young men grow into adults and leaders, these lessons will become integral to their daily lives, and they become givers of their own Ultimate Gifts.

## An Invitation

Are you ready to make a meaningful difference in your community and nurture stronger bonds with your son? Whether you're inspired by the incredible work of the Young Men's Service League or the profound lessons of Jim Stovall's *The Ultimate Gift*, there are numerous ways you can get involved and start creating positive change today.

Next Steps:

1. **Join the Journey:** Become a part of the YMSL family by volunteering your time, skills, and compassion. Whether you're a mother looking to strengthen your bond with your son or a young man eager to make a difference, YMSL offers opportunities to contribute to your community while growing as an individual.

2. **Read the Book or Watch the Movie *The Ultimate Gift*:** If you haven't already, pick up a copy of *The Ultimate Gift* or set time aside to watch the movie and discover the transformative power of its lessons. Let its wisdom inspire you to lead a life filled with empathy, compassion, and a commitment to serving others.

3. **Apply the Lessons:** Take the principles from *The Ultimate Gift* and apply them in your daily life. Small acts of kindness and service can profoundly impact those around you and the world. Start today, and be the change you want to see.

4. **Share the Message:** Spread the word about YMSL and *The Ultimate Gift.* Tell your friends, family, and colleagues about the positive work being done by YMSL and the life-changing lessons in the book. Please encourage them to get involved or explore these valuable teachings.

5. **Support YMSL:** If you cannot volunteer your time, consider supporting YMSL financially or donating resources. Your contribution can help YMSL continue its mission of fostering stronger bonds, serving communities, and promoting leadership.

Remember, it's never too late to embark on a journey of service, personal growth, and making a lasting impact on the lives of others. Join us in pursuing a world where empathy, compassion, and a generous spirit are the guiding principles that shape our communities and families.

Together, we can create a brighter future for all. Get involved, embrace the lessons of *The Ultimate Gift,* and let your actions be the ultimate gift to the world.

Email: **UltimateGift@ymslnational.org**
Phone: 1-866-602-9675 (YMSL)

# Introduction

## How The Ultimate Gift Comes to Life
## at the Young Men's Service League (YMSL)

### Introduction to YMSL's Ultimate Gift Journey

Before we dive into the heartwarming stories of the young men and their Ultimate Gift Project experiences, let's take a peek behind the scenes at how these transformative projects come to life at YMSL.

### The Genesis of Transformation: Understanding the Ultimate Gift Projects

A successful YMSL Ultimate Gift Project has two equally important goals that require careful balancing. First, we aim to foster a genuine bond between the young men, their mothers, and the individuals they serve. We emphasize understanding the "WHO" – the people and communities benefiting from our philanthropic efforts. Our goal is for our members to connect with those they serve. Second, the Ultimate Gift involves hands-on work in partnership with our chosen philanthropy. Similar to Red Stevens in the original story of *The Ultimate Gift*, our projects aim to create a significant impact for philanthropies who might not have the resources to achieve these changes independently. The challenge is achieving both goals while designing a chapter's Ultimate Gift.

### Leadership and Vision: Steering the Ultimate Gift Towards Success

Each chapter annually appoints an Ultimate Gift Chair and an Ultimate Gift Committee. The ideal Ultimate Gift Chair is a passionate mom with solid project management and leadership skills. The Ultimate Gift committee, comprising three to eight YMSL moms, reports to the chapter's Vice President of Philanthropy. They are responsible for identifying the Ultimate Gift recipient and bringing the project to fruition.

Communities and philanthropic partners fall into various service categories, each with its unique needs:

- Food Insecure
- Homeless
- Families in Need
- Veterans/Military/Public Safety
- Senior Citizens
- People Living with Disabilities
- Environmental Protection

Through the dedicated leadership and vision of these committed individuals, YMSL ensures that each Ultimate Gift project is thoughtfully crafted and executed, effectively addressing the diverse needs of our communities and making a lasting impact in the lives of those we serve.

## Selecting and Executing the Ultimate Gift

Having established the framework of leadership and commitment within each chapter, we now transition to the heart of the matter by taking a dream to reality. Our plans and intentions take shape in this critical phase, transforming abstract ideas into tangible actions that deeply resonate within our communities.

The initial step in this transformative journey involves carefully selecting the community and philanthropic partners for the Ultimate Gift, each distinct in their service categories and specific needs. We assist the philanthropy in identifying projects by walking through a series of questions designed to help inspire them about their "dream needs" and changes that would significantly improve their organization and consequently impact the community they serve.

Once the committee has gathered submissions and potential candidates for the Ultimate Gift Project, they face the daunting task of selecting the recipient community for the year. The decision-making process involves assessing the viability of the Ultimate Gift Project in terms of available work, hours required, and whether it can accommodate busy schedules. The chapter then presents its plan to its board of directors before seeking approval from National YMSL to ensure alignment with the Ultimate Gift's goals.

Simultaneously, the committee educates the chapter about the chosen service community and its unique challenges. This education serves a dual purpose: it refreshes the story of the Ultimate Gift's inspiration, reminding members of the book and movie by Jim Stovall, and connects their hearts and minds with the people they will serve.

Upon completion of the Ultimate Gift, the Chair and her committee provide a debriefing report summarizing the outcomes and serving as a valuable resource for future leaders. Chapters often create tribute videos that capture community education and the impact made on our philanthropic partners.

Now that you've gained insights into the inner workings of our Ultimate Gift projects, I invite you to delve into the stories that showcase the profound impact YMSL has on our young men and the philanthropies with which we partner. Whether you're considering joining our organization, represent a non-profit seeking support, or are an individual or corporation looking to give back, we invite you to connect with the Young Men's Service League. As you read through these stories, remember that the Ultimate Gift Project and YMSL continue to thrive, making the world a better place, one act of service at a time.

*Please Note: The introduction to each story has been written by Jim Stovall. The "Gifts" highlighted in this book refer to the original 12 Gifts that were identified in The Ultimate Gift story.*

# THE GIFT OF WORK

**"He who loves his work never labors."**

*"One of the things my wealth has robbed from you and the entire family is the privilege and satisfaction that comes from doing an honest day's work."*

— The Ultimate Gift

# A Homecoming to Remember

Garrett reflects on his experience in welcoming home those who served our country in the military. He shares recollections of an event that I believe will impact you as much as it has impacted me. Amid the sacrifices our service members make, it's often easy to overlook that their entire family shares their sacrifice.

When I was Garrett's age, young servicemen and women were returning from the Vietnam War. Unfortunately, many of the disapproving feelings and beliefs about that conflict were projected onto our returning veterans. I am grateful that today, there are efforts to offer those Vietnam veterans recognition for the service they gave decades ago. Thanks to young men like Garrett, our returning service members will receive the gratitude and appreciation they deserve as a well-earned part of their homecoming.

## GARRETT CLINE | North Dallas Chapter (Texas)

*My name is Garrett Cline, and as a senior at Richardson High School, I was honored to serve as President of the North Dallas Chapter of YMSL in 2011. Out of all the remarkable work our chapter accomplished and the countless hours of service we were proud to offer, welcoming our deployed soldiers was by far the most gratifying and humbling experience. Though I cannot speak from experience serving in the military, I'm sure that the separation and sacrifice of a deployed soldier must be almost unbearable for both those away serving their country and the families waiting patiently at home, knowing how happy they will be when they can reunite after a long tour. My mother and I cherished these reunions most during my time with the YMSL because we loved ensuring that our heroes felt the warmth and gratitude they deserved when stepping back onto U.S. soil.*

*During one of the many times we were fortunate enough to be part of a "Welcome Home" crowd at the Dallas-Fort Worth International Airport, we arrived early and took our places amongst the eager men, women, and children in the baggage claim. We could feel the electricity in the air. Our troops were coming home. As we craned our necks to look out over the crowd, I suddenly heard something next to me that sounded like a whimper. When I looked down, I noticed a young woman leaning into a stroller to gaze at her newborn baby boy. Her smile was contagious, and it immediately occurred to me that we were about to witness something truly breathtaking. Nudging my mother, she turned her gaze, and without exchanging words, we locked eyes. I could tell we were quickly becoming emotional as we realized this little one was about to meet his father.*

*One by one, the soldiers began to trickle through the terminal and were quickly met with embraces, firm handshakes, and smiles. For some, a deluge of tears marked the shoulders of soldiers' fatigues. I glanced back at the young mother and her child, and her face lit up. She finally saw him coming around the corner behind the ocean of military uniforms. My mother and I held rapt attention—his tear-filled wife with their newborn in hand had been waiting so long for this exact moment. As they made eye contact, he dropped his bags and ran straight to his family. He kissed his wife, took his son in his arms, and as he raised his baby in the air, all the stress of deployment, the sleepless nights, and the fog of war dissipated. He was now a father.*

*My mother grabbed my arm and put her head on my shoulder. There seemed to be continuity in the fact that my mother and I could connect in this moment while witnessing a lifelong bond forming between a father and son. Looking back, I'll never forget that soldier and his family. It was an amazing spectacle of love and sacrifice that many will never understand.*

*In these moments, we are reminded of brave men and women who overcame and weathered so much adversity to protect and serve our nation. I also think back to the YMSL and how they allowed us to engage with our community in many unbelievable ways. While this is only one story about my time with the group, the experiences I collected during my tenure undoubtedly shaped the man I am today. I am eternally grateful for that.*

# Another Brother

In the midst of his Ultimate Gift project, Calvin found an unexpected opportunity to serve, and through that service, he forged an unforgettable bond. His efforts culminated in a hug of gratitude that sealed that special moment with his new little brother.

## CALVIN WALLS | Mission Chapter (Texas)

*I participated in the Believe It Foundation's inaugural Miles for Smiles event. The Believe It Foundation provided adaptive bikes to individuals with physical disabilities, allowing these kids to ride a bike like their peers. Miles for Smiles is an event where the children could ride or, if needed, be assisted in riding bikes on a two-mile course through SeaWorld.*

*When I arrived at the event, we all prepped the route and set up the track for the kids. As the kids showed up, we helped them get to the starting line to prepare for the ride. Additionally, people were needed to help push the bikes of many of the kids as they could not ride on their own.*

*The kids who could not ride on their own had severe autism. One kid didn't have someone to push his bike for him and was looking around, trying to catch his mother's eye because of how uncomfortable he was in that situation. I pointed him out to one of the adults heading the event and walked over to help and be the younger kid's buddy. When I asked the kid's name, he told me it was "Nathan." I was shocked. It was the same name as my little brother. A connection formed in my mind right then and there, and I promised myself I would give this kid the best experience possible.*

*I pushed Nathan for the next two miles around the course and watched his excitement grow throughout the race. I will never forget when Nathan told me to go faster, and I could hear the joy and glee in his voice as we sped up.*

*As we got to the end of the route, I saw Nathan's mom crying as she watched me push her child. She had a look of disbelief because, as I found out later, she had never seen Nathan be comfortable enough to function or have fun without her or her husband with him. It was an incredibly emotional atmosphere that, I felt, moved me permanently. The small act of pushing their child for two miles at SeaWorld brought the family to tears of joy. You never know how a small act of kindness can really help somebody, and even going out of your way to do something small can tremendously impact that person's life.*

*After the event ended, while Nathan was leaving with his parents, the mother led Nathan back to me and told me how much she appreciated what I did, and Nathan gave me a big hug. It was a small moment of gratitude, but it was able to transmit the incredible emotions they were experiencing. The whole event left me with a feeling of gratitude. I could feel the gratitude radiating off the parents and Nathan. I myself felt gratitude for being able to participate in this event that helped so many parents.*

# Happy Holidays

Nothing is more memorable or exciting for kids than toys during the holidays in December. In his Ultimate Gift project, Andrew was reminded that, for many among us who are less fortunate, toys are a challenge for both kids and parents. Andrew and his fellow volunteers helped connect the right toy with the right child for the right parent. In this holiday equation, one-plus-one-plus-one can equal millions, and the words "Happy Holidays" are more than a greeting; they come to life.

## ANDREW WRIGHT | West U Chapter (Texas)

*I volunteered with my peers during Christmas break at the Houston Children's Charity morning toy distribution. It was a lively Christmas morning in Houston at the event, but I had no idea what to expect. While driving to the event, my knees started to shake in the car for some reason, and I didn't know why. I felt nervous, but it was the type of nerves you get before going on a roller coaster ride. When we arrived, I saw many toys in boxes and in different groups. Once we arrived, they immediately told us what to do. I was told to go move a stack of girl dolls over. There were at least two hundred boxes. I was so irritated until they gave me some help. While moving the boxes, I talked to one of the officers. He said this is a massive drive that occurs annually, and only a few people come out to volunteer. I started feeling much better after he told me how special the annual toy drive was to many children, and I worked harder to ensure the event went smoothly. Before they arrived, they gave us instructions,* and then I became even more excited. We were instructed to give each family a stuffed animal and a board game.

For every kid I encountered, I had to help them pick out gifts. With fifteen minutes to shop, I started thinking how fun this would be. After the instructions, they warned us they might be aggressive. As they opened the door for the first group, it was like a bunch of bees leaving their nest and attacking a bear after stealing their honey. They came in there, running, pushing, and shoving each other. My friend Darnell and I spotted someone in the middle of the stampede who needed help. We immediately saw her and went to help her. She seemed to be overwhelmed by what was happening.

I asked how many kids she had, and she said she had seven. Immediately, I tried to figure out how to get her as fast as possible because they only had 15 minutes to shop. She told us the ages of her kids, and Darnell and I split up to maximize our time. He went to the teenager section, and I went to the little boy's area to pick out monster trucks and other fun five-year-old boys' toys. Once we helped her, we took her to the checkout. That's when I saw the smile on her face, and it made me realize how important it was to them. After I helped her, I felt so happy and accomplished that I ran over to help other people to ensure they were getting the toys they needed and were having a good time overall.

After helping my first customer, I realized I needed to help as many people as possible. I ran around looking for someone and saw someone who looked confused and needed help. She had three girls, and her time was running out. I asked her how many toys she needed. She said she has twelve toys. We went through all the toys, looking for dolls and makeup kits. I made sure that it was perfect just for her kids. After we found all of her gifts, we started talking, and she said that this toy drive is significant because it helps parents with lower incomes provide their kids with presents for Christmas morning. After that, I hugged her and told her I was glad to help her and hoped she had a MERRY CHRISTMAS. That experience changed my life. I remember the special moments I had as a kid on Christmas morning, and I felt honored to be a part *of another kid's special morning. My parents have always taught me the importance of giving to others, but that morning, I learned a valuable lesson: the gift of giving is more powerful when you help others give to someone they love.*

# Pride of Place

Through his Ultimate Gift project, Connor discovered that everyone needs a clean, safe place to live and grow. This is particularly true for those who have dealt with the devastation of domestic violence and abuse. As Connor was improving the living conditions for women and children needing a safe place to recover and regroup, he determined what kind of man he wanted to be in the future. It is powerful when we can help someone deal with their past and be inspired to a higher level for our own future.

## CONNOR SCHLEGEL | North Star Chapter (Texas)

*For my YMSL Chapter's Ultimate Gift in 2022, I had the opportunity to serve multiple times at Emily's Place, a shelter for women and children. The facility badly needed help with landscaping, repairs, and the installation of safety features on their playground. I was excited about the project because I knew I would enjoy working outside, building with my hands, and serving alongside my YMSL friends. What I didn't realize was how powerfully the experience would impact me. I've always understood the terrible truth of domestic violence and child abuse, but hearing the leaders of Emily's Place talk about the awful conditions the women and children there have endured before fleeing from domestic violence and other horrible situations helped me understand the impact I could have by serving there.*

*When I first arrived at the shelter, I immediately realized how protected these beautiful families were with a full-time security guard and the blessing of* an unlisted residence. The heavy security made me face the harsh reality of what the residents had gone through—that they had finally escaped their abuse and often left their homes with nothing. I felt proud to have the chance to help them, to help make the needed improvements so that all the kids who come to Emily's Place would have the opportunity to feel happy and play on a playground I helped build.

I collected and delivered needed supplies to the property, and then we mowed and renovated the lawn. Several playground structures were old and unsafe, so we rebuilt or repaired and secured the equipment, installed many cubic yards of rubber pellets, and made the playground a safe space for the young girls and boys staying at the residence. I loved the experience of putting hard work into a task that would benefit not only the current members at Emily's Place but all of the desperate families who would come looking for a fresh start in the future. The most touching moment of my time working for the Ultimate Gift was seeing a little boy, no older than six, running out on that playground to experience the normal childhood he deserved. Knowing that my efforts that day would, in some small part, bring joy to these children and their loving mothers was the Ultimate Gift I could ever experience.

I was extremely fortunate that I was able to serve multiple times at Emily's Place to finish these projects. I knew I would enjoy the experience, but I didn't expect how working at the shelter would change me. Helping these women felt like I was giving back to all the amazing women who cared for me when I was growing up. The women in our lives give everything to protect and provide for their families; the women at Emily's Place left everything behind to help their children escape from the very people who should have protected them.

It made me consider the kind of man I want to be. I would never want to be a man someone would run from, but I get to choose to be a man who can build a safe space for others. I can be the kind of man who protects and stands up for those who can't do it for themselves. I was blessed to have participated in the Ultimate Gift and incredibly thankful for Emily's Place for providing needed services to these women and children.

# THE GIFT OF MONEY

**"Money is nothing more than a tool. It can be a force for good, a force for evil, or simply be idle."**

*"There is absolutely nothing that can replace money in the things that money does, but regarding the rest of the things in the world, money is absolutely useless. For example, all the money in the world won't buy you one more day of life."*

— The Ultimate Gift

# The Gift of Generations

Among the many shortcomings in our society today is the lack of respect for the generations that have gone before us. We learn life's lessons through experience. We can gain knowledge through our own experiences, but we have access to unlimited wisdom in the experiences of the senior citizens around us.

Through his Ultimate Gift project, Tye discovered the power of generations through working with senior citizens, growing to appreciate his mother, and even observing a bird with babies in a nest.

## TYE HOLDRIDGE | Keller Chapter (Texas)

*Dear Mr. Stovall,*

*My name is Tye Holdridge. I am a sophomore at Keller High School and a member of the Keller Chapter of the Young Men's Service League. Our Ultimate Gift this year was a service project with Whitley Place Senior Living Residence. It was an unforgettable project that we boys and our moms worked together on, something we called "Gather the Generations." This experience was a gift to me to see the world around me through the lens of the lessons of The Ultimate Gift book.*

*As a member of YMSL, the Ultimate Gift meant so much to me as I got to sign up and give the gift of a perfect day to the residents of Whitley Place, especially having the gift of time with my mom. Building that relationship with my mom and doing things with her really made me grateful for how amazing* she is as a mother, how she really influences me, and how she makes me a better person. I could see the gift of love that was put into the project from the beginning planning stages until the final celebration. In her, I saw the power of kindness, and she showed me our purpose: that small actions make a big difference in the life of another.

Our community was so generous in donations and helping make the project happen. Together, my mom and I saw firsthand the gift of giving. During my volunteer work, I saw the gift of work and the pride of a job well done, too.

We came together to renovate their Whitley Place home by cleaning up the yards and trimming trees. We also found a hidden bird's nest with a mom and her babies. This was a perfect way to remind us of the gift of gathering together. In another activity, we put together a veterans' parade called "Salute to Service." It was led by the Keller drumline, with everyone following behind them, waving flags and yelling, "Thank you for your service!" Their smiles meant the world to us as they watched from their windows, and some were all bundled up in the cold weather. In those moments, I saw the gift of gratitude.

Many residents became ill during Thanksgiving and had to be quarantined, so our plans for a fall festival halted. Instead, I helped make care packages for each resident to remind them they were not alone. This adversity presented a gift to us all to force a change in our course, to teach us not to give up, and to show us that, even in uncertain times, we can still do good things for others.

With the gift of friends, I helped build two wheelchair-friendly picnic tables so that all the residents could gather and join their families when they visited. We helped Whitley Place enjoy the gift of family. We also created a game room for the residents to play games together and spend time with one another. On many Sundays, I joined the residents for ice cream sundaes. I served some ice cream for them and watched them light up with joy as we poured some sprinkles on their orders. No matter your age, everyone loves chocolate and sprinkles. It is the little things that make the world a better place.

*One of my favorite days at Whitley Place was Game Day, when we played bingo and various games with the residents. I brought out the cornhole and the bags, and I was tossing by myself. Then, the sweetest lady ever came over to me. I introduced myself, and so did she. She asked to toss a few, and then we played with each other. My goodness, she was just insane at cornhole. I would miss the whole board, and there Ms. Jo was, draining them left and right with the biggest smile on her face. She whooped me each round. Ms. Jo winning each time was definitely the gift of laughter. I spent a lot of time visiting with Ms. Jo. Her advice to me about life was to "hang loose and it will all work out." In those moments with her, she shared the gift of learning. I learned she was an accountant, an Alpine ski instructor, and raced. I could tell from the get-go she was very smart and had a competitive fire. Of all the accomplishments she had in her lifetime, her greatest pride was her son. She told me, "He's a jewel." I saw the love she had for her son is the same way my mom loves me.*

*One of my favorite parts of our Ultimate Gift was making a story box for Ms. Jo to represent her life's story. The look on her face when she opened her box was priceless. She could see that every little piece I made for her was a part of her life. She could hardly believe that I remembered her stories or would take the time to make this especially for her, but most of all, I really listened to her story. My time with Ms. Jo showed me that a lot of adventures happen in a person's lifetime. I learned that we all have a story that is made up of all the people we meet along the way and all that we do. I came to understand the gift of time given to others is meant to be meaningful and have purpose. When I began the project, I thought that I was giving "The Ultimate Gift" to Whitley Place, but I realized that the gifts were actually given to me.*

*What surprised me during this experience was how easy it is to make such a big impact. Since I had never done an event like this, I was led to believe that making such a big impact would take a lot of people, time, money, materials, and many other different things. In reality, it only took a group of high school boys, amazing moms, boxes, food, and a little bit of time. All of these simple things led to a dramatic change for children in need in my community.*

# Homeless in My Hometown

Hope, giving, and love always come full circle. I am amazed and grateful that, as a blind person myself, I sat in a small office in my hometown of Tulsa, Oklahoma, and dictated a book that created an impact around the world, generated a major motion picture, and prompted a young man like Michael to serve the homeless right here in my hometown. Michael came to understand that homeless people are individuals just like you and me who have fallen victim to a few circumstances that shattered their world. With little more than the desire to make a difference, we can impact homeless people and, as Michael discovered, be impacted ourselves.

## MICHAEL PIELSTICKER | Tulsa Midtown Chapter (Oklahoma)

*Night Light Tulsa meets each Thursday night under a bridge downtown, where they set up a number of stations to serve the homeless population of Tulsa. I planned to hand out food, therefore physically nourishing those who truly needed it. It had been a few years since I had volunteered for the program, and my past experiences had not been fantastic. The last few times I had gone, it was freezing cold, and I was generally uncomfortable. It was one of my least favorite charities I had served, and I had no intentions of returning. However, my experience at the charity on December 10th was wildly different. It started like I remember from before, unloading trucks and setting up each station. Then came time for the staff to assign each person to a job. Though I had intended to hand out food, I was not allowed to do so, so I had to pick a different job. I* decided to help at the "blessings" station, where I gave out small toiletries and other necessities to those who needed them.

The biggest difference between my most recent experience and my prior experiences at Night Light was my reaction to the people I was serving. The staff members stated before we started that they hoped our experience under the bridge "messed us up in a good way." The experience certainly messed me up by seriously skewing my perception of homelessness, as many of those experiencing homelessness looked like those who would be members of my family or my friends. There was no divide separating us except for our financial circumstances. They were just normal people living out their lives like me.

Everyone who came to our station was exceedingly grateful for the items we were giving out. Seeing people so grateful for something we consider trivial was uplifting and humbling. This shows how we should be grateful for everything we have in life, down to the smallest blessings. Volunteering here allowed me to love and serve others like Jesus did during his time on Earth.

When I served, there was a sense of community that allowed me to be in unity with many people that I would typically not interact with regularly. I pray that I gave those I helped hope for a better future and that they can overcome whatever may be afflicting them now.

I met many good people while I served, but no one had more impact on me than a woman named Ederia. She first arrived at the station and handed me a small pocketbook of important Bible verses to remember, which I was grateful for. I was shocked that I had come to give out items to others and that they were giving me items in return. However, this was not the greatest gift that Ederia gave me that night.

One of the staff members wanted to introduce her to me, and so she returned later to talk to me further. Each time that she is introduced to a new person, she asks them one question, "If you could meet Jesus and had two words to say to him, what two words would you say?" She asked me this question, and I took a few seconds of time to think and then responded with, "Yes, Lord." When she heard my response, she began to cry. She said that she was deeply *moved by such a young person's faith and obedience to Christ. She asked my mom if she could pray for me and gave one of the greatest prayers I had ever heard, praying for my protection and the continuation of my faith. I truly believe that I gained more from this experience than I gave out to others.*

# Teamwork Makes the Difference

In this Ultimate Gift project, Eric combined his efforts with other volunteers to prove the wisdom of the ancient adage, "Many hands make light work." Eric also discovered that many of the veterans he helped would team up to assist one another or simply provide encouragement and friendship. Eric's experience reminds us all that freedom isn't free, and those who have gone before paid the price for the life we live.

## ERIC GOU | Alpharetta Chapter (Georgia)

*In my Ultimate Gift project, I helped on the Veterans Empowerment Organization campus by loading mulch for their garden, painting the fence in their yard, and painting the mural at the entrance of their campus. Other kids were helping by staining the deck and the chairs and tables on the campus. My favorite thing was helping my friend paint the fence and mural, probably because it required the least manual labor.*

*The Veterans Empowerment Organization helps homeless or struggling veterans who have trouble transitioning into society. We help make their living space cleaner and show them that there are more people who care about them and are willing to help them get back on track. I've learned that veterans who come off the battlefield may not have the resources or the skills available to be able to find jobs. Some of these veterans suffer from various injuries, be it physical injuries or mental injuries like post-traumatic stress disorder, substance abuse, depression, or anxiety, that would prevent them from securing* a job and lead to homelessness. For example, I met a resident who was blind in one eye and another who was almost deaf in an ear. I was even able to talk to a few veterans living there. They all expressed their gratefulness for our help.

I remember I talked to two residents who were good friends. One of them was extremely talkative and told me stories about his deployment in the Navy. The other wasn't so talkative, but I learned that they were pretty close because one of them was not allowed to leave the campus grounds for a while during the hours they were open. I think it was for leaving the grounds for too long or for another reason that I forgot. So, the talkative one would get the other person to do shopping for him. It was really nice to be able to get to talk to them because I realized that there were, as obvious as it sounds, people within their community willing to help each other. Even though many volunteers are willing to help these veterans, I'm still honestly surprised that not many people realize that those who fight and put their lives on the line for our country often struggle to transition from the battlefield and fit in society.

# A Tradition of Giving

Giving can become a habit, a routine, or an ongoing part of our daily lives. When Tomas described giving as being in his family's DNA, I realized he had been raised in a giving culture. His Ultimate Gift project made a lasting difference for a group of special needs kids, but I know Tomas's legacy will be a lifetime of giving that he will pass on to his family.

## TOMAS RETANA | First in Flight Chapter (North Carolina)

*Dear Mr. Stovall,*

*My name is Tomas Retana. I am a YMSL First in Flight Chapter member in Raleigh, North Carolina. I am currently a junior at St. David's School. Service is in my family's DNA. Ever since I can remember, we have been engaged in different philanthropies. Joining the Young Men's Service League felt very natural to me. Every year, I wait with excitement to hear about The Ultimate Gift, as it is the team's most significant activity and has a great impact on my community.*

*This year's recipient of the Ultimate Gift was Fox Road Elementary School, a magnet school located in the South of Raleigh. At first, I was surprised we had chosen a smaller project than in previous years. However, when I heard the demographics of the school, how more than 60% of the children in this school fall below the poverty lines, how the only daily meal they have is at school, and the only time spent outside is during school hours, I knew this would be the greatest of experiences.*

*We would have a tremendous impact on the kids and the community. Our project had three main activities: creating an outdoor playground for kids with special needs, renovating and enhancing the current outdoor area, and remodeling the teachers' lounge. The project kept growing because of new ideas from the team. We painted murals, created sensory walls, planted flowers, built a fountain, built sandboxes, made the teachers' lounge cozy and filled it with supplies, etc.*

*I was responsible for building the sensory walls. This project allowed me to develop creative thinking. I researched what could be included to stimulate kids with special needs. Knowing that the kids in this school only spend time outside when here, I wanted to make their experience unique, memorable, and with a purpose.*

*We built four multi-sensory environments with different textures, colors, and sounds for interactive and fun play. Each wall was unique, and although we encountered many obstacles (for example, how to make pots and pans stay on the wall), we never gave up. We knew we were working to provide a group of underprivileged, special needs kids with the opportunity to engage in this learning experience. We all worked hard for many hours, researching, buying, or collecting the artifacts and designing the wall.*

*During this project, I also picked up leadership and motivational skills. Despite the issues, we kept encouraging and empowering each other. We firmly believe that all children should have the opportunity to be outside, play, and learn. This project made me realize the things we take for granted, how blessed we are, and how we always need to be grateful.*

*When we finished the project, I stood in silence, admiring in awe the work we did, how beautiful it looked, and how much the kids and teachers would enjoy their new environment. I saw many smiley and proud faces, and my heart was full. Serving this group of kids meant a lot to me. Just imagining the daily joy of these special needs kids makes me see the importance and impact of our Ultimate Gift.*

# THE GIFT OF FRIENDS

**"It is a wealthy person indeed who calculates riches not in gold but in friends."**

*"Friend is a word that is thrown around far too easily by people who don't know the meaning of it."*

— The Ultimate Gift

# From Mundane to Memories

Nash learned a powerful lesson as he served some very special young people. His Ultimate Gift project proved that what could otherwise be a boring, mundane task becomes a memorable life experience when done in the service of others. Nothing makes us feel more special than making someone else feel special.

## NASH WILLIAMSON | Highland Park Chapter (Texas)

*Dear Jim,*

*My name is Nash Williamson. I am a freshman at Highland Park High School and a member of a Highland Park YMSL group in Dallas. Last year, I volunteered for the program Young Life Capernaum to serve our local Dallas special needs community.*

*Children with special needs come to the Young Life Capernaum meetings to express their creativity, show off their talents, and, most importantly, develop friendships with each other. Throughout three meetings, I was tasked with caretaking, teaching, performing on stage concerning each night's theme, and setting up. However, my decision to volunteer was secretly a blessing in disguise, as the seemingly mundane tasks soon became heartwarming memories.*

*On the first meeting, I walked over to a boy playing ping-pong alone. Everyone else seemed to be having a blast goofing off with their friends and playing games. But it was almost like he was in his own little bubble of isolation. His body language told me he was sad, so I offered to play with him. His face lit up with excitement! He was jumping with glee. We played a couple of rounds until a little girl came over to join in. We began switching off with each other so she could participate as well. Then, after another handful of rounds, other kids began to surround the ping-pong table and wanted to join in as well.*

*The girl handed me her paddle, and we played one last match with the crowd of kids watching. It was almost like we were in a Wimbledon tournament! It would've been wrong not to let him win in front of the crowd, and so he smoked me. The crowd exploded with cheering. It even drew the attention of the kids playing mini-basketball from across the room. Kids swarmed him, wanting to be the next one to play him. Not only did he now have a crowd of superfans, but he also now had a crowd of friends.*

*Suddenly, they called for everyone to return to the theater room, and I watched as kids eagerly followed him and sat with him. Before he turned a corner, I caught a glimpse of them having a group hug. Then it hit me. It made me realize that Young Life is about making special needs kids feel like they belong.*

*Although this was just one of the many ultimate gift moments I experienced at Young Life, it stood out to me like a sore thumb for this very reason. What I would give to experience this memory for the first time again!*

# A Little Time Goes a Long Way

While I am always grateful when young men like Jackson express their gratitude to me for my book and the inspiration it gave them to serve in their communities, I am quick to recognize and point out that my book, *The Ultimate Gift*, and the movie based on it, were fiction. The commitment that the young men and their mothers in YMSL made to serve others is real. Through his project, Jackson came to understand that while products and services can help people, the gift of time shared with others can create the most lasting difference.

## JACKSON COLE WHITCOMB | Four Points Chapter (Texas)

*Dear Jim,*

*Thank you for giving us this opportunity to share an experience of serving others. My name is Jackson Whitcomb, and I am currently the Vice President of the Four Points Chapter of YMSL in Austin, Texas. I am a junior at Hyde Park High School, and it's my third year serving in YMSL.*

*This year, we had the opportunity to serve through Drive a Senior, Northwest Austin. Since I recently got my driver's license, it was a strong reminder that driving is a privilege. I took local senior citizens to social events and doctor appointments while learning a little about their former careers, grandkids, and ailments. Soon, I realized that the conversation was as much of a gift to my elders as the transportation. These senior citizens have not only lost their freedom but also lost their ability to socialize.*

*Two of the most meaningful seniors I served did not even ride with me as they were homebound. One client needed me to stand in line at the local food bank for her. I woke up early to get the "best" produce per her request and lined up in a church parking lot. As I patiently waited my turn, the volunteers smiled and chatted with me, not knowing that I was usually the one on the other side of the table. I was humbled and pleasantly surprised at how warm and welcoming they all were as we dug through the produce together to find pieces of fruit that had the fewest bruises. When I delivered the groceries, the client quickly accepted my offer to unpack and store the items. She was so thankful and seemed pleased I asked to stay and chat with her awhile as I asked her questions about herself to extend the conversation.*

*Another gentleman who made a significant impact on me had gradually gone blind and deaf. I communicated through his sister to learn when to go to his home to receive a credit card and grocery list. He was waiting for me as promised and was very trusting to hand me his list and credit card, which made me realize how much he needed to depend on others. I shopped for his exact list and asked his sister if I could add some of his favorite treats at my own expense. His sister was so thankful and explained that she had been taking care of him herself for many years. Having someone else make a grocery trip here and there was such a gift to them both.*

*Seeing the isolation and limited abilities of seniors has made me realize how important it is to take care of each other right here in our own neighborhoods. I have become a better conversationalist and will try to take a little more time with all the seniors I come across, including my own grandparents!*

# A Clean Start

Nikhi was like most of us who believe our day starts when we take a shower and prepare for the day. Our worldview shifts, as Nikhi's did, when we come to understand that, for many people, a morning shower is not something to be taken for granted. Coming to recognize this reality helped Nikhi to find pride, dignity, and a sense of community service in the mundane task of cleaning a bathroom.

## NIKHI KURIAKOSE | Cardinal Chapter (Texas)

*My name is Nikhi Kuriakose, a freshman at Lovejoy High School and a member of the Cardinal Chapter YMSL. I joined YMSL the summer before ninth grade. My school chapter was full, so I joined a neighboring chapter, allowing me to grow my community and expand my service opportunities.*

*One charity I immensely enjoyed participating in was Streetside Showers. This experience in the Texas summer was eye-opening and humbling. This organization has mobile shower stalls that provide a shower and personal hygiene care for those without a home or access to water. I helped clean the inside of the showers and bathroom after each use and also refilled the bottles of soap, shampoo, and conditioner as well as provided new, clean clothes. I ensured that the mobile bathroom was sanitized for the next person to use by wiping all surfaces and spraying disinfecting spray throughout the area.*

*This service is important because it gives the people without homes or access to water something to look forward to and helps them to be clean. It gives* community members without resources a chance to refresh, and this clean start is a seed of hope. It is the ultimate gift to help plant this seed.

When I first arrived at Streetside Showers, I was reluctant to participate. It is a three-hour project, and it was Texas summer heat outside, nearing 100 degrees. The line of individuals who were waiting just to take a shower made me realize quickly that this service is very important. It is a lifeline to hope and dignity, and it made me also realize how lucky I am to have access to basic services and to all the things that I have.

I enjoyed this experience because I like helping people who need and want assistance. I met people who didn't have half the things that I have, yet they are happy and thankful, teaching me to be grateful and humble. Although I thought this event was going to be boring, it turned out to be a wonderful experience not only for the community but also for me. It was an experience that I won't soon forget. Not only did the individuals that I assisted benefit from this experience, but I did, too. I learned that people are the same regardless of their circumstances, and a shower and a clean start is the beginning of pride and hope.

I realize that living with uncertainty and fear is real in our community after serving at Streetside Showers. I appreciate the people in my community who do not have access to the same resources and privileges as I do, showing me their joy and hope. I am glad that I could help those in need and be part of their journey to dignity and hope through this Ultimate Gift project.

# A Flight of Honor

Recently, my 92-year-old uncle passed away after living a long and successful life of service and achievement. One of the highlights of his last year on earth was taking an Honor Flight from his home in Florida to Washington, DC. He got to experience our nation's capital and see the monuments honoring his service and the memorials to his comrades in arms who made the ultimate sacrifice. It was indeed the trip of a lifetime, but when he described the eventful day to me, what stood out most in his mind were the countless people in Florida and Washington, DC, who came out to thank him for serving our country. Connor, through his Ultimate Gift project, provided this element of gratitude and respect to those who made our freedom a reality.

## CONNOR KWAN | Dulles Chapter (Virginia)

*Dear Jim,*

*My name is Connor Kwan, and I am a member of the Dulles Chapter of YMSL and a sophomore at Lightridge High School. My Ultimate Gift was participating in an Honor Flight that departed from Dulles International Airport for Vietnam and World War II veterans. Honor Flights are flights that gather veterans from across the country to visit our nation's memorials in Washington, DC, for a day to celebrate their accomplishments. Most of the veterans who took part in the flight fought in a war for the U.S. Every Honor Flight is coordinated by a non-profit organization, and many of the volunteers were members of organizations like YMSL.*

*In preparation for the Honor Flight, I created signs that thanked the veterans for their service and purchased American flags to wave during their departure. After a couple of days, I, along with dozens of other volunteers, lined up along the terminal hallway as we prepared to cheer for the veterans. When the veterans' departure started, we cheered them on and thanked them for their service. The veterans were mainly elderly, as the wars they fought occurred decades ago. Each had a helper walking with them, most of whom were their kids. As I watched them walk by, I realized how much they sacrificed for our freedom. Some were missing limbs, while some were in wheelchairs.*

*One veteran came up to us and told us that this was the first time he ever felt truly appreciated. Another veteran was taking videos and saying he felt like a celebrity. This made me feel happy as I was able to make a difference in someone's life, no matter how small the act was. The whole Honor Flight showed the veterans that people cared about them and their sacrifices; it made them feel like they fought for something valuable. Soon, the first set of veterans entered the plane, and I found out there would be a second wave coming in an hour.*

*This hour in between was just enough time to grab food and a drink. Then, the second wave of veterans started. Their reactions were about the same as the first set of veterans. However, this time, one of the helpers came to thank us. She told us that the recognition meant a lot coming from younger people because it made the veterans feel like their story was passed on to a new generation. Overall, the Honor Flight made me realize that I haven't taken advantage of the freedom given to me by the veterans.*

*Throughout this experience, I witnessed the effects of showing compassion and empathy. The veterans were people who needed to have their achievements and sacrifices acknowledged. Volunteering gave me the ability to do this, and I'm grateful for the opportunity to make a difference in someone's life. It gave me a deeper understanding and appreciation for the sacrifices made by veterans and the importance of honoring their service. For the veterans, the Honor Flight provided a sense of recognition and appreciation for their service, as well as a chance to reconnect with their military past and share their experiences with others. Additionally, it gave the veterans a chance to visit the memorials in Washington, DC, that honor their service, which can be a powerful and emotional experience.*

# THE GIFT OF LEARNING

"Education is a lifelong journey whose
destination expands as you travel."

*"The desire and hunger for education is the key to real learning."*

— The Ultimate Gift

# The Gift of Time

As a blind person myself, I have a sense of understanding regarding what parents of special needs kids go through. It's an all-day, everyday struggle just to care for and meet the needs of a child. Rudra, the young men who served with him, and their moms made it possible for a group of special needs kids to have a wonderful experience and allow their parents some time to simply rest and relax. Rudra discovered the wisdom that the best activity you can provide for anyone is simply to be their friend.

## RUDRA SHARMA | Pleasanton Chapter (California)

*My name is Rudra Sharma. I am a freshman at Foothill High School and a member of the YMSL Pleasanton Chapter. Our Ultimate Gift project took place in December, and the event's goal was to provide respite for parents of kids with special needs. The event was split into three main parts. Some volunteers arrived early to sort all the gifts and set up the venue. Others were part of the activity crew, which headed all the activities and provided buddies for the kids. Finally, a few helped with the tear-down crew and took everything apart. I volunteered to be part of all three crews and saw first-hand how our efforts helped people.*

*The setup crew came one day in advance and planned how the event would run. My mom and I signed up because we needed the volunteering hours, and I ended up being the only boy volunteer to help with this task. I helped the moms running the events sort out all the gifts, organize the tables' layout, and set up* a place for the parents to relax. It was a blessing because it allowed me to gain the trust of the moms and understand how much effort goes into planning and organizing an event like this.

I signed up to run the craft crew with other volunteers on the event day. I was able to plan the activities on the station and quickly adapt to the needs of the children visiting them. On my last shift, I signed up to be a buddy for one of the kids. My buddy was very sweet and eager to do things with me. I helped him make cookies, play games, and pick out gifts for the rest of his family.

After spending two hours with him, I realized just how much effort it takes to care for a kid with special needs. I was in complete awe of the patience and love the parents gave their children, and the least I could do was give some love and time back.

Finally, when the event ended, I stayed back to help the tear-down crew. We packed up the activities and cleaned up the venue. I was tired after volunteering the entire day, but I felt accomplished. I finally realized that what the kids needed wasn't someone to take care of them but a friend who could spend time with them. I am grateful to have had this experience, and I have gained a newfound respect for kids who don't have the same opportunities that I do. I saw the true meaning of the Ultimate Gift and helped many families have a better Christmas.

# Enjoying a Great Meal

Maxwell serves as a reminder to us all, both in America and around the world. While we may live and work in a comfortable environment, countless people in the 21st century face the age-old struggle of simply getting enough food to eat each day.

As he was performing the tedious task of assembling meals, he found himself energized as he thought of the people who would be fed by his efforts. His desire to find a path where he can make a similar contribution to the world throughout his life is what YMSL and *The Ultimate Gift* are all about.

## MAXWELL MONTES | Las Vegas Chapter (Nevada)

*Dear Jim,*

*My name is Maxwell Montes. I am a junior at Coronado High School and a member of the Las Vegas chapter of YMSL. Our Ultimate Gift project last year was assembling, packing, and shipping thousands of meals to underprivileged and hungry children in the Las Vegas area through the organization Serving Our Kids.*

*Although these children are provided with school breakfasts and lunches, that only covers five days of the week. These meals were for the weekend when these children frequently went hungry. The project was two hours of physically demanding work in a hot warehouse doing repetitive food packing in the form of an assembly line. Whenever I began to get bored of the work, I just visualized a less than fortunate child waiting for a good meal, and I would work even harder.*

*Although the experience only lasted for two hours, the rewards lasted exponentially. When I got home that night, our dinner was a usual one, but it tasted so much better—not because it was different, but because of the children I couldn't get out of my head after every bite. Meals are so much more precious to me now than before the charity event. I used to treat a meal like it was just a part of my life, but now I think of each one as a gift.*

*Though it tasted better, it was hard to chew and swallow. The image of the model hungry child kept popping up in my head as I ate, and I couldn't help but think that not only was that one child hungry for the meal I ate, but there were thousands of others who were hungry in my city. As the days went on, I thought about how I could only supply them with one meal while I supplied myself with three every day since then.*

*Deep down, I know there's nothing else I can do besides volunteer, but it has only given me more motivation to volunteer and do good in my community. Not only that, but I feel like I want my life to somewhat contribute to these issues in a positive light, to work in a field that benefits the less fortunate and where I measure my true wealth in the lives I impact and not in dollars. Doing charity work creates a symbiotic relationship between the giver and the receiver. Everyone benefits at the end of the day, and that is what matters to me.*

# The Roots of Service

Zachary outlines the statistics that clearly indicate food insecurity is a reality within our country today. These numbers show that, even in the richest country on the planet, getting enough to eat each day is a struggle for many families among us. But all the statistics in the world can't tell the story that one hungry person can share. Zachary and his fellow volunteers made a permanent difference as they created tables that will be used to prepare and provide vegetables for hungry people in the community for many years to come.

## ZACHARY HEISCHMAN | Prosper Chapter (Texas)

*Dear Mr. Stovall,*

*My name is Zachary Heischman, and I'm a senior at Prosper High School. My mom and I are with the Prosper YMSL Chapter. Since this is my fourth year with YMSL, I've had the opportunity to participate in several Ultimate Gift projects, but the one that stood out for me was in January/February 2021. I was a sophomore and had a year under my belt serving the community. I didn't fully understand the impact I was having yet, and, to be honest, probably didn't think too hard about it.*

*McKinney Roots is now a Texan by Nature Certified Project! Texan by Nature Project Certification provides Texas employers, organizations, and individuals with recognition of meaningful conservation efforts involving and benefiting people, prosperity, and natural resources. It was a relatively new philanthropy organization for our chapter, but it stood out. The first time I did volunteer work there was in the middle of summer, and it was scorching hot! The Texas heat is unrelenting, but I walked away feeling invigorated because we had just harvested so many amazing vegetables from their organic garden. This was a blessing for the local food pantries because people were now able to get some fresh vegetables and fruits that they had not been able to get before.*

*The opportunity to do Ultimate Gift was an experience that gave me a fresh perspective on how food insecurity existed in our area. McKinney, Texas, is just around the corner from my home, but the statistic for food insecurity was an eye-opener. Sixteen percent of McKinney families struggle to provide meals for themselves and their families. In McKinney, 9.8 % of children are below the poverty line, and 7,600 children qualify for free and reduced meal programs. With five acres of land to garden, McKinney Roots will see a significant improvement in physical health for all participating community members.*

*Our Ultimate Gift project was to build vegetable tables for which the newly harvested vegetables can be cleaned and dried. Our chapter built these tables from the ground up. Many of us learned how to measure, cut wood, and assemble the tables for the first time. It was a lot of trial and error because we had never done it before, and some didn't know how to use some of the tools. Nevertheless, it was a great experience because McKinney Roots can now utilize these tables to do what they need done.*

*In subsequent visits to McKinney Roots, these tables were still being used, and I can proudly say that our chapter was responsible for making that happen. The best part is knowing that future groups who volunteer at McKinney Roots will benefit from the vegetable tables that we built to help the organization.*

# Challenges and Abilities

Through his own physical challenge, James was able to bring a powerful and positive perspective to the young people he served in his Ultimate Gift project. As a blind person myself, I understand the significance of benefiting from someone else's example of overcoming their own physical differences. I have found that regardless of where we want to go, we can all reach our goals, but some of us have to take a slightly different path. James understands that we must be committed to our mission but flexible in our method.

## JAMES A. BUTLIN | Vienna-Oakton Chapter (Virginia)

*A favorite activity I have discovered through my involvement with the Young Men's Service League (YMSL) has been volunteering to support kids with disabilities. As an amputee, though, I've discovered that I'm not big on labeling people as "disabled," which implies limitations or a broken state (as in a car is "disabled" when it is not working). As a competitor in advanced academics and multiple sports, I much prefer overcoming obstacles, breaking barriers, and challenging stereotypes.*

*My first exposure to the Down Syndrome Association of Northern Virginia (DSANV) was last July when my mom and I signed up to run Friday night bingo. It had gone virtual to keep the kids connected during the COVID-19 pandemic. True, I missed a party with my high school friends to run the game from our dining room table, but it was totally worth it. I loved engaging with the kids on those "Zoom boxes" as they asked what sports I played and liked best. It was clear that they had already formed friendships with each other through other DSANV gatherings and were BINGO pros; in this game, I was the novice. We laughed together as my mom and I scrambled to come up with fun, age-appropriate words to say aloud so the kids could check their scorecards and cover their squares ("B-7. B as in balloon, baseball, bumpy, 7"). So, when I learned YMSL's Ultimate Gift would be supporting DSANV Field Day on October 2, 2022, I was quick to register!*

*Field Day was to follow the annual Buddy Walk and serve as a celebration for the kids with Down syndrome and their families and supporters throughout the region. On the drive over, I assumed that the morning rain had put a damper on the event, but this couldn't have been further from the truth. We quickly transitioned the field day activity stations indoors. I observed dozens of enthusiastic kids, family members, and volunteers hugging, laughing, and socializing as though it was the most beautiful day of the year! I happily received my assignment to man the tattoo station, and I specifically remember lots of requests for temporary tattoo stickers related to Sesame Street and sports themes. I recognized some of the kids from BINGO night, and they recognized me. At one point, I got dragged over to another station for a "dance party" and then into a photo booth with crazy props (I still have the photo).*

*Putting smiles on the kids' faces by simply being engaged and fully present was a refreshing and rewarding experience for me. Their enthusiasm and sincerity helped me put things into perspective, too. No one asked why my leg looks different, how "it" happened, or what I can or can't do with my prosthesis. We just enjoyed spending time together with no expectations, judgments, or questions. Participating in this YMSL Ultimate Gift experience made me wonder what else I might be able to do with my special gifts and blessings to help and learn from others. It also reminded me that I need to sign up for more Friday night BINGO!*

# THE GIFT OF PROBLEMS

**"Problems can only be avoided by exercising good judgment. Good judgment can only be gained by experiencing life's problems."**

*"When we can learn from our own problems, we begin to deal with life. When we can learn from other people's problems, we begin to master life."*

— The Ultimate Gift

# A Bit of Sunshine

In the midst of helping young people enjoy a ropes course, canoeing, and an overnight camping adventure, Roman came to realize that, more than creating a moment or a weekend experience, he was helping to create memories for kids and their families. As invariably happens through Ultimate Gift projects and community service, Roman realized that he received far more than he gave when all was said and done.

## ROMAN RAWIE | Hills of Westlake Chapter (Texas)

This past summer, I volunteered with an organization called Austin Sunshine Camps (ASC), a group founded in 1928 whose mission is to provide the magic of overnight camp to local kids at no cost to parents. ASC bases its work and fun activities from a historic wooden clubhouse tucked away in a corner of Austin's famous Zilker Park.

This summer was one of my favorite volunteering experiences: interacting with campers while helping at events like canoe night, carnival night, and even at the camp's very own version of the Austin City Limits music festival. When I look back on the summer, I'm very happy that my YMSL chapter, Hills of Westlake, decided to partner with ASC for our Ultimate Gift project. Some of our chapter's activities were working check-in and clean-up duties and the ropes course at ASC's family day, a time when campers shared the excitement of camp with their parents or caregivers. Our group also teamed up that afternoon to put together storage cabinets for shoes, backpacks, and other campers' items.

*During the family day, I witnessed the joy in one camper as she held her grandmother's hand while walking around the property. Her grandmother was smiling widely as she spoke quickly to her granddaughter. The girl responded excitedly with a similar bright smile as they talked about the games and the counselors she knew so well. I also saw a look of total pride on a camper's face when he struggled to eventually make it to the top of the two-story ropes course. His dad was also very proud seeing his son make it so far up. But my best moment of the day was watching a scene of peace and complete happiness as a camper held his full family's attention while they sat together at a picnic table. Everyone in this memory was all ears as the camper happily described the meals, projects, and good times he experienced during his time at ASC. His family seemed amazed to hear about all the things their son had done at the very same picnic table while a camper at ASC.*

*On the surface, our Ultimate Gift project was a group of young men and our moms providing time and labor to complete small projects or staff-up events for which the camp needed volunteers. It was actually a lot more than that for me. Through this special day, I watched as kids happily showed their families that they could be expert tour guides about a place they knew and loved. I observed how parents and caregivers enjoyed this quality time with their children while they also had a chance to be kids again. Even though we were volunteer workers for the event, I feel like I actually received a memorable payment. The opportunity to help support kids and their families enjoy a new experience in a beautiful outdoor setting touched my heart and is something I think about often. Without question, I received much more from my volunteer time at ASC than I was asked to give.*

# Ringing the Bell

Kaleb discovered the heart of the matter when we do community service or anything else in life. What we do, how we do it, where we do it, or when we do it is insignificant until we get in touch with why we are performing a task and who we are serving. A doorbell is a fairly simple, insignificant device until you come to understand what it can mean to someone and how it can improve the way they live.

## KALEB DANIEL STONE | Tulsa Midtown Chapter (Oklahoma)

*As I woke up that crisp December morning, put on my shirt, and grabbed a handful of lattes for the crew, I couldn't have anticipated the rewarding journey that day would kickstart. I volunteered with Meals on Wheels, meeting with friends from school to clean up an elderly woman's yard and install a new doorbell system before deciding to go to several more homes to install more doorbell systems. I wasn't expecting much when I got there, but we had a good time volunteering together, so we kept going; however, as the number of times you do service piles up, you start to forget why you do it.*

*You become numb to service when you don't even know why you're doing it. As Christmas drew closer and the hours piled up, I wanted to remember why I started doing this service in the first place. This persisted until the last time we went out to install doorbells when something different happened. We were installing a doorbell at an old retirement community at the home of a woman who lived alone. We knocked on the door, but she wasn't there, so we went straight to work. When we were nearly done, one of her neighbors saw what we were doing. He came over to us and said how the woman who lived there had poor hearing and often missed when guests came over because she couldn't hear them. He told us how thankful she would be that someone was willing to help her, and now she'd be able to know when guests arrived.*

*As we left, I reflected on this simple comment, turning it over in my head. I had never realized how much such a small act of kindness could bring such a genuine response, even if relatively mild. I had always thought that people tended to brush off these small things, taking a negative view of many people to appreciate things, especially if it doesn't directly benefit them. This, I think, is why I would so often become quickly burned out or disillusioned when I volunteered often; however, now, I had a much less negative view once I began turning this simple moment in my mind.*

*As Christmas came and went, and I saw the happy and charitable face of the world when they turn to their families for even a brief moment, I saw people in a light I hadn't been able to see previously. I saw people more charitably; I saw people more positively; I saw my fellow man as partners in making a better community. This instilled in me a new drive to serve that I hadn't had previously. I delved headfirst into my duties at YMSL, working to do what I could in the time I had to try and create those little acts, those seemingly small things that make an impact beyond what might be expected. My time serving in and through YMSL has been one of the most rewarding experiences of my life, especially volunteering with Meals on Wheels during the Christmas season. I will always be thankful for that experience, and I hope, with deep sincerity, that I can keep this desire with me throughout all my days.*

# Different but the Same

In the aftermath of his Ultimate Gift service projects, Carson shares the wisdom he gained, which is far beyond his years. We are, indeed, all from different circumstances with different backgrounds and different abilities, but in our hearts and souls, we are very much the same. We can't choose what happens to us in this life, but we can always choose what we're going to do about it.

## CARSON DOKE | McKinney Chapter (Texas)

*Everyone is different in their own way, but at the same time, we are all the same. All of us are human; we all have souls and personalities. What sets us apart from one another is the cards we are dealt. We are all dealt different cards, and what we choose to do with those cards is what makes us who we are. Some are luckier than others. Some are born with disabilities or are born into poverty. Life is not easy if you're dealt difficult cards. We should help one another by doing whatever we are capable of. We are all on this adventure we call life, and it isn't always fair. A little kindness can make a huge difference in the lives of others.*

*The goal of our YMSL Ultimate Gift is to provide kindness to those who need it most. I have had the opportunity to be involved with two different Ultimate Gifts. The first Ultimate Gift I volunteered with served Incredible Fridays. Incredible Fridays provides respite care for parents of children with special needs, also known as incredible kids. Parents drop their children off for four hours, knowing they are safe and being cared for, giving the parents much-needed time to have a date night, run errands, or just relax.*

*Our Incredible Friday's Ultimate Gift was to host an "incredible" Christmas Party for the incredible kids and their siblings. It was a magical event with games, crafts, snowball fights, and Santa. Each kid went home with a special, personalized Christmas gift from Santa. Our members collected the gifts, wrapped the gifts, prepped crafts, made snowballs, made games and photo booth props, decorated for the event, and were buddies to the incredible kids. All the kids had an amazing time; they had an incredible night.*

*The second Ultimate Gift I participated in benefited Shiloh Place. Shiloh Place gives homeless single mothers a free place to live for two years. They supply the families with all their groceries and toiletries while teaching them skills so that they can provide for themselves.*

*Our Shiloh Place Ultimate Gift was to refresh the playground and host a fall festival for the families. Our members power washed and stained the fence, play structure, benches, and porch swing. We installed play-safe landscape edging and repaired and replaced various elements of the play structure. Additionally, we built giant lawn games and a covered storage area for the residents' bicycles and riding toys. We also held a family-friendly fall festival for the residents of Shiloh Place, where we unveiled the refreshed play space. The kids had fun at the fall festival, and the parents were thankful that we were able to create a safe place for their kids to play.*

*While volunteering at these places, I saw firsthand what the people there had to deal with. Seeing these things makes you more understanding and sympathetic towards others. It made me grateful for the cards that I was dealt and opened my heart to help others. With our Ultimate Gift, not only did I see these things, but I also got to experience them.*

*During our chapter's Shiloh Place Ultimate Gift reveal, I was given a scenario where I was a single mother with an extremely limited income, and I had to budget all of my expenses for a month. It is truly a tough decision to cut things out of your budget that you need but cannot afford. At the Incredible*

*Friday's reveal, I sat in a wheelchair while balancing a lunch tray on my lap and navigating through obstacles. I realized how hard it was and how much I took walking for granted. These were extremely humbling experiences. Millions of people have to make difficult decisions and complete difficult tasks every day.*

*As I said, we're all different, yet we are all the same. The cards we've been dealt aren't always fair, but what we choose to do with our cards is what puts us on our path. Sometimes, a little kindness and support can completely change someone's life. If we all put in a little time and effort into helping others, humanity could dominate this adventure that we call life.*

# Making a House a Home

One of the fastest ways to improve how people feel about themselves is to change their environment. Turning a barren house into a warm and welcoming home doesn't just change the environment; it changes people. In the process of transforming a living space, Sam began to transform himself when he discovered serving others is not just what we do but who we are. I appreciate the fact that Sam challenges the rest of us to join him on a lifelong Ultimate Gift journey.

## SAM DARE | First in Flight Chapter (North Carolina)

*Dear Mr. Stovall,*

*I'm Sam Dare, a junior at Green Hope High School in Cary, North Carolina, and a third-year member of YMSL. In 2021, my YMSL chapter, First in Flight, worked with an organization called Passage Home Inc. to renovate a communal space for an underprivileged community in Raleigh and a home used as transitional housing for families in need. For the house, the whole chapter pitched in with painting, power washing, and cleaning the exterior. Then, chapter members and local businesses donated spare furniture sets, tables, couches, televisions, stands, and more until the house was full and ready to be occupied. My family donated a flatscreen TV. Lastly, we cleaned the house and stocked it with food. Meanwhile, the communal space was a mess. Weeds had overgrown it, and there was detritus and debris all over. So we got to work weeding the garden, replacing an open-air stage in the space that was rotting* and tilted, renovating the sandbox and other play areas, and removing large tires that had been buried in the area.

Once everything was complete, it was immensely gratifying to see how our hard work had paid off. The house, a messy, blank slate, had been turned into a cozy, comfortable home for struggling families. Once dirty, overgrown, and dank, the communal space was now orderly, refurbished, and ready for play again. It struck me how much of a difference this made in people's lives. When the community members came out and saw it, their smiles just proved it even more. But after it was complete, it was just done. We went back to our area, back to volunteering in our usual charities, and what my chapter had done slipped my mind.

With YMSL, changing people's lives is so ordinary that something like what we did can simply be just a stepping stone to a greater, bigger project, but it's important never to forget each and every project. But that's just what I did... until I got an email from my Chapter President asking if I could edit the video of our Ultimate Gift to submit to Nationals. I had tried my hand at video editing before, so I accepted, willing to do what I could to help the chapter. When I edited that video, going back over all the photos of smiling kids and their moms, hardworking young men pulling weeds or moving furniture, time-lapses of the house, and communal space being reborn, it all washed back over me. Seeing how happy and content everyone was and knowing they were working for a good cause brought warmth to my heart. For my video to be the best it could be, I decided to get a few interviews from community members and volunteers with Passage Home Inc. Seeing how overjoyed they were to hear from one of our members months later and hearing them gush about how much of an impact we made on their lives, it solidified it for me.

When I originally started YMSL, I thought volunteering would make me feel more satisfied and happy. But what I have learned, which is so strange about volunteering, is that it is a way of life. Helping others at the expense of your own time, body, and wallet brings a sense of completeness that nothing has ever given me. It is so easy to make such an immense impact on people. You can *sacrifice a couple of hours of your time to make someone's month. In our case, our whole chapter sacrificed about a week or two of our time to change a whole community's life. I truly believe volunteering to help others is the single best thing one can do to positively impact the world. Don't believe me? Go try it.*

**In loving memory**: Sam Dare's inspiring journey of service ended tragically in a car accident before this book's release, yet his spirit lives on through his impactful work and the people he touched. In honoring Sam, let's embrace his call to action –"go try it"- transforming our sorrow into positive change and continuing his legacy of kindness and community service.

# THE GIFT OF FAMILY

**"Some people are born into wonderful families, while others have to find or create them."**

*"Being a member of a family is a priceless privilege which costs nothing but love."*

— The Ultimate Gift

# Our Daily Bread

Even with the myriad of worthwhile nonprofit organizations and faith-based institutions, there are gaps in the safety net that provides the basic essentials for those among us who are less fortunate. Mark discovered through his Ultimate Gift project that, while it's wonderful to have organizations that provide food for the needy six days a week, people still need to eat on the seventh day. As he became aware of the needs in his own community, Mark discovered that community service is a never-ending way of life.

## MARK WANG | Lake Oswego Chapter (Oregon)

*During the week, from Monday to Saturday, churches normally give out free meals to homeless people. However, on Sundays, there is a gap. As such, the mission of Potluck in the Park is to fill that gap by providing a hot meal every Sunday, all 52 weeks of the year, no matter the weather. This is the story of Potluck in the Park, a Portland-based philanthropy organization.*

*In December last year, I had an opportunity to work with this organization for the YMSL Ultimate Gift project. My mom took me to their office located in downtown Portland. There, we met with more volunteers. I learned that our task was to help renovate their reception room. I was assigned to the painting work. It was the first time I ever painted a house. I got paint on my hair and clothing, but I painted a new layer onto the ceiling and wall. My fellow volunteers and the staff at Potluck in the Park were very nice and helpful to me.*

*They taught me how to paint and encouraged me along the way. All this time, I felt a sense of pride that I was doing something great for a good cause.*

*What surprised me most is that there were so many homeless people showing up for the meal. I never had to worry about being hungry in my life, and that's something I have taken for granted. This area is only 20 minutes away from my home and school, yet there are so many people struggling with poverty. Food security is still such an urgent issue in my city. I am happy that I am aware of it now and am doing something to help solve the problem. Now that I have a better picture of the homelessness issue in Oregon, I can start to fully appreciate organizations like Potluck in the Park and the work they do to help these people. There are still a lot of people who need help and free meals, and Potluck in the Park will need my assistance. With only a little effort, I can change the lives of many people for the better.*

*When I heard about the story of Potluck in the Park, I felt inspired that people were willing to spend their precious time to help others and to make their lives better. It's heartwarming to think that despite how uncaring the world can be at times, there are always groups like Potluck in the Park who are willing to help you back onto your feet.*

# The Power of a Fence

A well-built fence can increase the value and beauty of a property while defining a space and creating a safe place within. Fences have long been used in literature and lore as symbols. One of my heroes, Mark Twain, used a fence as an object lesson in his classic novel, *The Adventures of Tom Sawyer*. In my own book and movie, *The Ultimate Gift*, I wrote about a young man building a fence on a ranch as the first lesson in his ultimate gift quest. Cooper and his Young Men's Service League co-laborers performed many tasks to improve a special place and then worked on the fence around it to make it safe and secure.

## COOPER ANDREOSKY | Pleasanton Chapter (California)

*Our Ultimate Gift event was held at the Shepherd's Gate Foundation in November 2021. I worked with other volunteers to make a safer community for women and children. First, I became a lead stainer and painter. My guide was a former firefighter who taught me to stain fences (3 acres of them!), so I painted and stained all the fences around the perimeter with my buddies. We stained a lot of long urethane-saturated fences, or at least they are now. It took hours and days. After we finished the fences, I laid mulch onto the grounds so watered plants could hold the moisture longer and have fewer weeds.*

*We also did a little gardening, which was my favorite task. We planted vegetables. I think it was tomatoes, if I recall correctly. Once we finished planting and getting our hands dirty, we painted the curbs and gave them a fresh coat of "do not park here" red paint. It made the parking lot look new and cleaned up. We helped around the campus, picking up trash, planting flowers, and making it look beautiful for any newcomer arriving at Shepherd's Gate for the first time. They deserved a beautiful place to live. I then met some women and children who lived at Shepherd's Gate. They were talkative and super appreciative; one of their children even came and painted right next to us.*

*I helped the Shepherd's Gate women who were, at one time, abused, mistreated, addicted to drugs, put in a bad situation, or made poor choices where they ended up homeless and living on the streets. Because of what YMSL did, they have a safe place to get back on their feet and a beautiful, sheltered campus to recover. I think they appreciated all the work we did for them. They can come out to the gardens to read and relax. They have a safe space with no danger, and the areas we worked on reflect this new sense of tranquility. They also appreciated seeing young men and women, a community around them, willing to help rebuild them.*

*I learned that, at YMSL, it feels good to know you're helping people recover with your hands at work, in the dirt, in the paint, in the soil, and maybe even near the pain. I also learned how to become a leader as a more introverted person. It opened me to opportunities to help new people and teach them how to learn a skill, like staining or mulching.*

*I was surprised at how the women were put into these unfortunate situations. Their stories were super sad and painful, and it inspired me to give all my efforts to help them out in any way I could. I was astounded by how kind and open the Shepherd's Gate residents and staff were to us.*

*I loved volunteering at Shepherd's Gate because it improved their lives while it helped to improve my leadership skills and introverted self. I would volunteer there again. It was truly the Ultimate Gift. Thank you, Shepherd's Gate Foundation.*

# A Tiny Home Makes a Huge Difference

Through his Ultimate Gift project, Cameron learned that a home is far more than shelter from the elements. A home is a meaningful place of belonging and the beginning of becoming a part of a community and a society. Cameron and his fellow volunteers learned how to quickly turn building materials into tiny homes that will make a difference for vulnerable people for years to come. The old saying is indeed true: there's no place like home.

## CAMERON COLOMBE | Seattle Chapter (Washington)

*Our Ultimate Gift project for my sophomore year of high school was working with those experiencing homelessness by helping to build tiny homes and helping in the villages made up of tiny homes. I was involved with our chapter project from the beginning as I went to different locations to take pictures to document what our chapter would be experiencing during our Ultimate Gift project. While taking photos, I first went to the building where the tiny homes were being built. We met with the woman who designed the building process making it easier to keep up with the high demand for tiny homes in the Seattle area. I also went into a village where the completed tiny homes go. Seeing the tiny homes come together with other resources to support the people living there was eye-opening. It was explained to me that the success rate of keeping people off the street was because of the systems and resources set in place to allow for the villagers to have support for counseling and job placement. It was at this village that I saw how the people living there looked happy and proud to have a place called home. They had a community they could cook with, play with, and, most importantly, a dry place to sleep and a lock on their door to feel secure.*

*During the project, I got to go back to the warehouse and learn how to build a tiny home. I learned about pre-engineered jigs that allow a team of 10 to 12 people to build the shell of a tiny home in five hours, even if they have never built a house before. Learning to use a nail gun was exciting, but understanding that the house we just built would help get people off the streets was incredible. The homes we built as a chapter will impact up to 2,400 lives over the tiny homes' lifespan.*

*The entire process of our chapter's Ultimate Gift project made me realize that when a group of people come together, we can really make a difference on a very large scale that will impact others for many years to come. I initially thought I was just going to take pictures to help promote our chapter's Ultimate Gift with Low Income Housing Institute and their partner Sound Foundations NW, but I went home with a heart that wanted to learn more and do more to help others in need. This impacted me beyond just this project. I now try to volunteer as much as my schedule allows. This past school year, I did over four times the number of required volunteer hours. The Ultimate Gift and building of the tiny home inspired me to want to help out in our community more. I also realized that many of those who are experiencing homelessness need more than just a job to get their life back on track. They need a whole team of people helping them. They need a village! I was blessed to be a small piece of the village for a couple of weeks.*

# Beyond the Bench

In his Ultimate Gift project, Aidan worked to transform an outdoor area of an afterschool program and, in the process, uncovered some profound truths and transformed himself. He discovered that mundane and boring tasks take on new meaning when they are done for others. A bench can be a wonderful place to sit and rest, meet with friends, or simply enjoy a special day. Years from now, the benches Aiden created will be making a difference for others, and the process of creating the benches will be making a difference for Aidan.

## AIDAN MCFARLANE | Coppell Chapter (Texas)

*Dear Jim,*

*My name is Aidan McFarlane. I am a junior at Coppell High School and a member of the Coppell Chapter of YMSL. Our Ultimate Gift project last year was renovating the outdoor area of an afterschool program in an underprivileged area of Dallas called Voice of Hope. This renovation included repainting the whole fence black, constructing over 20 tables that folded into benches (what I was in charge of), the implementation of flower beds, and painting a white rectangle on the side of the building for a projector screen. As stated, I was leading the construction of the folding tables. While doing the same monotonous tasks of placing, drilling, and moving benches for three hours, not once did I want to leave or quit.*

*Why wouldn't the same arduous task not bore me for three hours? The answer was simple: The work at hand benefited something and someone greater than me. This work was benefiting not just a program but a community. This work was allowing an underprivileged community the space to gather as one and watch movies, play games, and enjoy each other. I was very surprised at the joy that came out of this project. Many of us were covered in paint, dirt, or had blisters from the work we did. But one thing that remained the same throughout every face of every mother and son was, believe it or not, a smile.*

*This project opened my eyes to what I shouldn't take for granted in my life. I was able to see that I am lucky to have multiple spaces like the one we built for Voice of Hope. Throughout the project, I was able to pick up leadership skills while also growing a newfound respect for the community we were serving. I am truly grateful for this opportunity, and I'm glad I was able to look past the confines of repetitive work in order to see the true meaning of our Ultimate Gift.*

# THE GIFT OF LAUGHTER

"Laughter is good medicine for the soul. Our world is desperately in need of more such medicine."

*"Many people live unhappy lives because they take things too seriously...*
*life without laughter is not worth living."*

— The Ultimate Gift

# Storage for Dreams

"Mac," through his Ultimate Gift project, solidified his understanding of the privileges he had been blessed with throughout his life and the fact that many other young people did not enjoy the same privileges. He and his YMSL brothers created an improved living space for foster kids, including a place to store their personal possessions. Having one's own space and a place to store personal possessions is among our basic human needs. By helping to provide this, Blake made a difference that will continue to serve others, and the lessons he learned will continue to guide him as he begins his career in the military and serves us all.

## BLAKE "MAC" STILLMAN | Prosper Chapter (Texas)

*Dear Jim,*

*My name is Blake "Mac" Stillman. I am a Senior at Rock Hill High School located in Prosper, Texas. In 2019, my brother Spencer (a junior) and I (a naive freshman) were only thinking about ourselves and how to navigate through our new high school. For two weeks, myself, Spencer, and other members of Prosper's Young Men's Service League (YMSL) chapter completed our Ultimate Gift project by supporting Journey to Dream (JTD). JTD is an organization for homeless teens with a Transitional Living Program for homeless youth working towards their independence. At first, I thought I was only giving my time, but soon realized I was receiving so much more by being a part of this awesome experience. I, along with several of my YMSL brothers, spent long days* completing cosmetic improvements to Kyle's Place, the JTD facility where 14 Texas teens lived.

All of us worked tirelessly alongside the Lowe's staff to build much-needed storage solutions to the six bedrooms the kids shared. This included refinishing 14 dressers, custom-built under-bed storage units, cubby systems for toiletries, shoes, medical binders, and mail, and refinishing their worn-out picnic tables. We set up workstations, and Lowe's team members guided us in our construction efforts. Our work ethic, positive attitude, and determination kept us going to ultimately surprise these foster kids when we revealed it all to them. Anyone of us could be in their shoes, and I believe our project helped bring awareness to me and my YMSL brothers. We have it made, and these kids without a home or family support system have a bad deal.

Our Ultimate Gift opened my eyes to Service Before Self. Today, the meaning of The Ultimate Gift resonates within me as a 2023 senior class member serving my final year in YMSL. I competed for and received Congressional Nominations to both The United States Air Force Academy and The United States Naval Academy to continue my commitment to Serve Before Self for our country.

I believe if you help a kid in foster care and open the eyes of a kid blessed like me, you change the world for the better.

# Gathering the Generations

One of the most significant depletion of natural resources in the world today is the ongoing loss of members of the Greatest Generation. People who lived through the Great Depression, World War II, and were a part of building the amazing society we enjoy today have wisdom and insight that can benefit us all. In his Ultimate Gift project, Brayden volunteered at an assisted living facility to make a difference for the residents. In the process, he discovered a treasure within the heart, mind, and spirit of his new 97-year-old friend.

## BRAYDEN DUNBAR | Keller Chapter (Texas)

*Hi, Mr. Stovall.*

*My name is Brayden Dunbar. I am a junior at Keller High School and a member of the YMSL Keller Chapter. This year, our Ultimate Gift's theme was "Gather the Generations," and we focused our efforts on helping Whitley Place, an assisted living and adult senior living center in Keller, with various projects.*

*I helped clean up the garden and hedge trees. I put together gifts for the residents and had the opportunity to interview one of the residents. Sitting down with 97-year-old Virgil Hughes and learning from his experiences was one of the greatest gifts of all. I never had the chance to meet my dad's father, and I lost my other grandfather almost two years ago, so it was great to sit down with Mr. Hughes and learn about his advice for all of us. My family supports our military, and Mr. Hughes served in the Navy. Even though there is an 80-*

*year age gap between the two of us, we found common interests—our love for the military and our families.*

*As I sat down with him and learned his life story, it occurred to me that one of the greatest gifts is not material things but life lessons we can learn when we "gather the generations." I am grateful to Mrs. Holdridge for putting together such an excellent way for us to support our community.*

# Caring for the Flag

All of us who are privileged to live in a free society owe a literal and a figurative debt of gratitude to those who have gone before who won our freedom and those who serve today to maintain it. In his Ultimate Gift project, Ketan made a difference for veterans, their families, and those who are currently serving us around the world. In the process of giving back to those who have made unimaginable sacrifices, he gained a better understanding of the debt we all owe, which can never be fully repaid.

## KETAN TAMIRISA | Lakes Chapter (Texas)

*Dear Jim,*

*My name is Ketan Tamirisa. I am a junior at Carroll High School and a dedicated member of the Lakes Chapter of YMSL. I was extremely fortunate to be able to take part in the Ultimate Gift project this year, which focused on honoring and serving veterans. This event was extremely unique in that it was held in partnership with the Travis Manion Foundation, which is a nonprofit organization that develops programs in order to empower veterans as well as families of fallen veterans. Throughout the course of the event, I was able to participate in various activities, including writing cards of appreciation to soldiers, organizing and transporting toys, taking time to self-reflect, and, lastly, learning the proper flag-folding etiquette.*

*One thing I learned through participating in this event is the value of putting others before yourself. I learned that it's imperative to take some time* out of your day in order to help better the lives of others around you, especially when they are sacrificing their safety for the protection of the country. Initially, it was difficult to understand the purpose of "rucking," or carrying, a heavy bag for about an hour in the cold December temperatures. However, as time went on, it became increasingly apparent that the underlying purpose behind the activity was to show our dedication to all of the veterans who are forced to carry heavy bags of ammunition and artillery day in and day out in order to serve our country. By the time we were finished rucking, I had developed a completely new mentality. I understood that dedication to a task and ultimate respect are the first steps to success.

After rucking, all the members of the different YMSL chapters came together and reflected for a couple of minutes near a serene pond. I thought that the location chosen for this activity was extremely conducive to self-introspection. After the five-minute period of reflection, I felt almost reinvigorated. Participating in this thought-evoking activity allowed me to take a step back and venture through the different avenues of my life in order to determine specific ways for me to better myself as well as others around me.

The last activity I am proud to say I was able to be a part of was learning how to fold and retire an American flag properly. Before we started folding flags, however, we were taught the history and significance of the flags themselves. I was surprised to learn that the flags are markers for the graves of fallen soldiers. They are, essentially, a symbol of bravery and determination and, therefore, necessitate proper treatment and care. Understanding this information helped to catalyze, for me, the process of learning how to fold the flags in the proper way, as I was able to do it after a couple of attempts.

Overall, through participation in these diverse events, I was able to benefit not only myself but the others around me. I was able to pay my respects to the war veterans and soldiers who have given their all for the protection of our country. I am blessed to have been able to be a part of this project.

# Art Imitates Life

As a blind person, I frequently am reminded of the absurdity of the fact that I write books I can't read that are turned into movies I can't watch. When a colleague in my office read Riley's story to me, I instantly realized he was the real-life embodiment of the character Jason Stevens I had written about in *The Ultimate Gift*, who later came to life on the movie screen. Jason's task in *The Ultimate Gift* was to build a fence, while Riley helped provide clothing and shoes for those less fortunate individuals in his community. For both young men, the project began as something that was required of them and had to be done. Then, enlightenment dawned on Jason and Riley as they embraced the cause and dedicated their efforts to making a difference.

## RILEY MCCAIN | Impact Frisco Chapter (Texas)

*Dear Jim:*

*I must admit, when I first heard about the Young Men's Service League (YMSL) from my mom, I was extremely confused. I knew that I had been sponsored into the program by a former member who saw potential in my ability to serve, but this carried a rather vague and intangible connotation in my young mind. When I eventually joined YMSL as a high school freshman in the midst of an ongoing global pandemic, my enthusiasm for the organization and its values was nonexistent. At that time, if I had been asked why I was a program member, my response would have been, "My mom made me do it."*

*As restrictions lifted and our area gradually returned to the halcyon days of pre-COVID joviality, YMSL service accordingly shifted from organizing the drop off of care packages on doorsteps to facilitating in-person events for the benefit of local philanthropies. After an extensive span of feeling isolated and disconnected from the community, I realized that this traditional form of service was a means in which one could see physical, concrete evidence of the impact he or she had on society. Although these in-person experiences greatly improved my appreciation for YMSL, my most significant eye-opening experience didn't arrive until the January 2022 edition of our chapter's Ultimate Gift project.*

*One night, as I was about to fall asleep, an email notification alerted me about an upcoming large-scale service endeavor for all YMSL members. "Ultimate Gift is on the calendar!" the message proclaimed. "Participation is strongly recommended!" Barely even glancing at the details of the project, I signed up for the event. After all, I needed to commit to another opportunity so that I could meet my annual twenty-service-hour requirement.*

*When the day finally came to show up and serve, the only thing on my mind as I entered the building was getting credit for my philanthropic actions. Our group was ushered into a common hallway, awaiting briefing on the tasks that laid ahead of us. Instead of merely outlining our assignments for the afternoon, the philanthropy representative began with a detailed description of not only the purpose and mission of the organization but also how our selfless assistance would ultimately lead to a positive outcome in our immediate local community. Awestruck, I learned that Frisco Threads, our YMSL chapter's 2022 Ultimate Gift partner, gives economically disadvantaged students and families in need around our school district the opportunity to select free clothing and/or shoes to ensure that they are dressed for success.*

*I had never considered the harsh reality that the clothing one wears to school has the potential to impact his or her educational experience and self-confidence—for better or for worse. Although the students our work would benefit remained anonymous and would select clothing privately at a later time,*

*I suddenly felt a passion to help these individuals by putting my best foot forward in regards to the quality of my personal mindset. Thoughts of service hours, requirements, and what I could have been doing on a Saturday afternoon were completely abandoned. I was no longer involved in YMSL to achieve a simple resume boost but to meaningfully and purposefully impact my community.*

*As the afternoon progressed, our duties included sorting clothing, building shelves, and organizing space that Frisco Threads could use to expand its clothes closet. Never once did the labor become tiresome or monotonous. Even though this work was not something one would typically consider "interesting" or "fun," touching the clothes that would ultimately change countless lives made the experience exponentially more authentic to me.*

*Leaving the building that day, I was genuinely proud of myself for giving my full and undivided attention to an important issue in our area. From that moment on, YMSL became less of a chore and more of a privilege. Not everyone has an opportunity to make a difference in the community. Even though I will never see the children we helped, I like to imagine that they are enjoying greater success in school and life as a result of our efforts to make clothing resources readily accessible.*

*Since our Ultimate Gift Day, I have returned to Frisco Threads several times this year to promote the continuity of our previous service. In addition, my family and I have gone through our own clothes, looking for donations that would benefit the program. I am genuinely grateful that our chapter's participation in the Ultimate Gift project not only connected me to an incredible philanthropy but aided in the development of a personal passion for service that will be a valuable asset for the rest of my life.*

# THE GIFT OF DREAMS

**"Faith is all that dreamers need to see into the future."**

*"Your dreams for your life must be yours. They cannot belong to someone else, and they must continue to grow and expand."*

— The Ultimate Gift

# A Myriad of Challenges and Opportunities

Through his Ultimate Gift community service project, Jared realized that there are an endless number of opportunities to serve and a wide variety of people who are in need. One of the great things about pursuing a life of service is that regardless of your talent, interest, or resources, there is a place for you to serve and people who need what you have to offer. Jared came to understand that there is no such thing as a stereotypical person in need. People who are facing challenges come from all walks of life and every conceivable circumstance.

## JARED AUSTIN FERRIS | North Dallas Chapter (Texas)

*I have had the opportunity to serve at a number of places across the Dallas area through YMSL, doing a variety of very different things. All of the philanthropies have been interesting in their own way, but the realization that people from all walks of life can use a helping hand at times became very apparent to me during one service event in particular.*

*In Dallas, there is an organization called the Stewpot, and they partner with The Bridge Homeless Assistance Center to serve meals to the homeless at their dining room called Second Chance Café. I volunteered to serve breakfast there one Thursday morning last summer. The café isn't anything special to look at, but I had a very special experience with the people that day. I was expecting to work on the serving line but ended up getting assigned to serve milk* and water to the people at the tables. This gave me a chance to interact more with the people than I would have on the serving line.

As I went to each different table, I had conversations with people whose situations and reasons for being there were all completely different. One table had a homeless lady who was a single mother who was struggling to raise her two kids. Sitting next to her was a man who was disabled, in a wheelchair, and couldn't work a regular job. At another table, I saw two young guys with backpacks. They didn't look much older than I am, so it seemed strange to me that they would be here with the others. After talking to them, I learned that they were actually college students! They were clean and well-dressed, yet they told me they were homeless.

I was blown away by the fact that despite being homeless, they were working their way through college to try and make a better life for themselves. I was so struck by this that it has changed my perception of all the people I have served since then. It made me realize that many different situations may lead to someone needing a helping hand and that all people deserve our respect.

# A Makeover of Giving

Often, in our youth, we are unaware of the issues surrounding aging and death that older people in our world face. Through his Ultimate Gift project, Max came to understand the void that is left behind when a husband dies and a widow faces life alone. Max was able to help fill that void and create a special anniversary while he came to a deeper understanding of the joy of giving.

## MAX KACERE | Tulsa Midtown Chapter (Oklahoma)

*One of the organizations YMSL partnered with this year for the Ultimate Gift project was Balcony Women. YMSL also partnered with Meals on Wheels, making ramps for elderly people, but since I did something similar last year, I decided to do the Balcony Women shift.*

*Balcony Women is an organization that simply builds up and encourages other women, specifically widows. I have to admit I was a little skeptical at what I could offer to help a widow, but it turned out to be profoundly moving and impactful. According to the National Institute of Health, there are 700,000 women who become widowed each year in the United States. A high percentage of them lose friendships, experience financial hardships, and oftentimes feel alone or depressed.*

*We had the honor to go to a sweet lady's home to do a variety of odd jobs. We painted her address numbers on the curb and did yard work, including cleaning out gutters, pulling weeds, and trimming bushes—which her husband used to always do. We also cleaned up her little outside patio area where she said she used to love to read and drink her tea, but since it's been a little neglected, she just hasn't done it lately.*

*I will never forget her face when she came outside to check on us. Her eyes filled with happy tears when she saw her little patio cleaned up and rearranged. She was smiling from ear to ear. I really felt like I was on a makeover show where the contestant starts crying and everyone is overjoyed. It was one of the best feelings I have ever had. It was amazing to witness, when I spent a little time helping someone else, how it actually had a bigger impact on me. I felt so much joy leaving her house that day. I remember telling my mom on the way home if volunteering was always like this, I would help out more often!*

*Thank you, Mr. Stovall, for sharing your book, The Ultimate Gift, with the world. It's because of you sharing your wisdom through this book that I had the unlikely, but sincerely appreciative, experience of serving someone I never would have otherwise. The representative with Balcony Women said that our sweet widow texted her and said, "These blessings are extra special because today would have been our 27th wedding anniversary. Sometimes HAPPY comes when it's least expected... thank you a gazillion times." This is what it's all about.*

# Giving and Receiving

Several years ago, I had a brief inspiration and spent five days in my office, between my phone calls and meetings, dictating what became *The Ultimate Gift* novel. That book spawned three more novels and a movie trilogy. Adam immediately identified one of the core messages I sought to create, and then he gave that message life through his actions. He describes how much he received through the process of giving and how he actually forgot he was serving others because it became so enjoyable and significant to him.

## ADAM GRAVELLE | Hills of Westlake Chapter (Texas)

*At the heart of Jim Stovall's novel Ultimate Gift is the lesson that giving brings even more joy and happiness than receiving. There is nowhere that reflects this more than Austin Sunshine Camps (ASC). As a volunteer at ASC, I have just as much fun as the young campers. At ASC training, we learned that many of the kids attending ASC have difficult situations at home, but having the opportunity to go to an overnight summer camp allows them to "look beyond their current situation and dream big." I didn't know what that really meant until I met the kids at ASC. It is a place of joy and fun where kids can just be kids, no matter their situation at home. I learned that I enjoy playing with and teaching young kids, and I had just as good a time as the campers.*

*ASC was one of the first places I volunteered when I joined YMSL, and I immediately fell in love with it. I didn't know exactly what to expect as I arrived at ASC on a hot summer evening. I dove right into carnival night, helping kids* play games and have as much fun as possible. I forgot I was volunteering because I was having so much fun with all the campers. They didn't talk to me like a volunteer but just another kid. Throughout the course of the summer, I also got to help with canoe night and Austin City Limits at ASC night.

I learned to be flexible and creative and to seek out those kids who were sitting alone to make sure they felt included. One carnival night, I noticed that a little boy was sitting alone looking nervous. I went over to sit with him and learned he didn't like the big crowd. He didn't want to play carnival games or do crafts. Through talking to him, I learned we had a common interest in basketball. We played basketball for hours, and I forgot I was volunteering and not just playing with a friend.

With fall and the start of school approaching, I was excited, but I was also sad to see the summer nights volunteering at ASC coming to a close. When I learned that our Ultimate Gift project would be putting on a family day at ASC, I couldn't wait to get started. We worked with the ASC volunteer coordinator to help plan Family Day to introduce potential campers and families to the fun of camp. We had 150 volunteers signed up, and we were ready to go.

The night before the big day, I got sick. I was so disappointed I wasn't allowed to volunteer in person, but I heard from my mom that Family Day was a huge success. Although I missed seeing families and caregivers get a small taste of the excitement of camp at Family Day, I will be back next summer volunteering and having just as much fun as the campers.

# Transformation with a Twist

Jonathan and his fellow Young Men's Service League volunteers had the privilege of serving veterans and their families who have sacrificed for us all. The volunteers also gained a new perspective on military service and our flag as our symbol of freedom. You've heard it said that to begin to understand another person, you need to walk a mile in their shoes. Jonathan began his Ultimate Gift project by walking two miles. Going the extra mile is a great way to serve and to live.

## JONATHAN JOSE | Lakes Chapter (Texas)

*Dear Jim,*

*My name is Jonathan Jose. I am a junior at Carroll Senior High School and a member of the Lakes Chapter of YMSL.*

*In the beginning of December 2022, I got to take part in one of the most transformative and engaging volunteer experiences of my lifetime. On a mild Sunday afternoon, young men and I from all grade levels of the Lakes Chapter gathered together under a park canopy, waiting to serve the Travis Manion Foundation. For those who don't know, the Travis Manion Foundation is an organization dedicated to providing support to military families around the nation, but more importantly, they educate young individuals like those in YMSL on how to truly appreciate, respect, and honor the red, white, and blue that has become an omnipresent symbol in our lives.*

*During the afternoon, we participated in a multitude of activities, each of them making me appreciate more and more what the brave souls of this country sacrifice on a daily basis for the protection of our daily freedom. We first donated and organized toys for donations to these military families but with a twist—a military twist. Led by a seasoned military veteran, we each grabbed a significant weight of toys and went for a two-mile walk, which represented only a fraction of the struggle that these military personnel had to go through in order to protect America. After we came back from the walk, though, is where the inspiration truly started to dawn upon me.*

*The next segment of our experience was one filled with solitude and reverence—how to properly dispose of the American flag. Before learning about the technical steps, we first sat down and listened to a deeply inspiring talk by the head of the operation, who described what the flag meant to him. Judging by the intensity and solemnness with which he spoke, it became increasingly apparent to me that the flag means so much more to people than a symbol of America. To different people, it could represent hope, opportunity, a lost loved one, a friend on the battlefield, and so much more. As I was listening to him spill his life story, I gained a greater appreciation of what it means to be an American and to wear those colors on my shirt. It wasn't a given; it was a privilege granted to me by those, past and present, who fought and sacrificed everything for our country.*

*After learning how to properly fold and dispose of an American flag, we made cards for the families of military veterans. In these cards, I made it my mission to emphasize how grateful I was to the individual as well as the family for the sacrifice they have given for the protection of civilians like me. Overall, the purpose of these cards was to display the gratitude and appreciation we had to these brave, loyal, and hardworking people.*

*To conclude, this experience taught me more than I could ever imagine. It gave me insight into what the American flag TRULY meant to the brave individuals of America. It opened my eyes to a part of our society I had never seen before, and it surprised me with the hardships and struggles veterans had to battle through before, during, and after their time in loyal service. It was an experience like no other, coupled with people like no other. That's the military who protects our lives every day. That's the frontline soldiers who sacrifice everything for the freedom and opportunity of this country.*

*That's the true emblem of the red, white, and blue. That's the United States of America.*

# THE GIFT OF GIVING

"One of the key principles in giving, is that the gift must be yours to give - either something you are, earned or created."

*"The only way you can truly get more out of life for yourself is to give part of yourself away."*

— The Ultimate Gift

# Home Sweet Home

Martin came to understand and appreciate the significance of the home and all the furnishings he has been given throughout his life. When we see people struggling for things we have taken for granted, we are filled with gratitude, which is the beginning of giving. The fastest way to get everything you want in life is to be thankful for what you already have.

## MARTIN ZSOKA | Silver Star Chapter (Texas)

*My name is Martin Zsoka. I am a Freshman at John Paul ll High School, and this is my first year in the Silver Star Chapter of YMSL in Plano, Texas.*

*This year, our chapter chose Bed Start as the Ultimate Gift philanthropy. It is such a wonderful opportunity for me to work with my friends while helping other people. For this project, we loaded furniture onto a truck, then delivered beds, sofas, and armchairs to people's new homes. This is basically helping them to move in. What touches me is to see their faces light up when they receive their new beds and furniture that quickly fill up their new apartment or house.*

*The best experience was around Thanksgiving when, besides bedding and furniture, some people donated food! With this donation, we knew that a family of six could have a complete Thanksgiving meal that evening. It was all in the kitchen—we delivered that, too!*

*To imagine that some of these people had to leave their native homes behind in dangerous countries like Venezuela and come to an unknown country, then receive friendship and love from strangers and get a new home is really a big thing! It makes me want to share and be willing to work for others to make them happy.*

*The other experience I will never forget is when we helped people restart their lives as they moved into a house where everybody gets one bedroom, and they share the kitchen and living room. We got to deliver all the furniture to this house, and while we were unloading, they already started to assemble the furniture we had just brought in. In this case, I felt so fortunate that my parents provide me with my own room full of everything I need, and I am able to help others have some of the things that they need! I know that God is always taking care of us, and I find this a way to show our love for others by helping them in their hard times.*

# Providing Through the Pandemic

When I write a book or create a movie, I simply want to tell a compelling story and leave a meaningful message. When people like Nathan, and the other young men highlighted in this book, take that message and bring it to life, I am filled with gratitude. My stories are little more than words on a page or pictures on a screen until people like Nathan make them a reality. He and his fellow volunteers found a way to stand in the gap for families during the difficult days of the pandemic.

## NATHAN H. GRAVELLE | Hills of Westlake Chapter (Texas)

*I joined the Young Men's Service League just as the COVID-19 pandemic began to shut everything down. My family was lucky because we had the essentials needed to get us through, but others in our community were not faring as well. A local Austin nonprofit we work with, Foundation Communities, provides affordable housing and on-site support services for families. During the pandemic, Foundation Communities was not receiving the help that it typically does. Individual donations were down, and social distancing requirements prevented volunteers from preparing living spaces and sorting donations. Our chapter reached out and learned the most immediate need was hygiene and household supply kits for resident families. We wanted to help.*

*Our big yearly project is called The Ultimate Gift as a tribute to Jim Stovall's novel. One of the tasks in the novel that particularly resonated with me was the gift of giving. Jason, the protagonist, learned that the more he gave of himself, the happier he became. As I thought about the gift of giving, I knew we could make a big impact by figuring out how to provide hygiene and household supply kits.*

*Foundation Communities families most needed diapers, so we worked with our local grocery store, HEB, to get as many diapers as possible. My mom and I wandered down the diaper aisle and asked the first HEB employee we saw, Sammy, if he could help us. He took us under his wing, helped us find bargain deals on diapers, and even used his time off and his own truck to transport the big boxes. Moms and sons gathered essential items like toothbrushes, soap, cleaning supplies, wipes, socks, and diapers. After gathering as many items as possible, we met in a parking lot to put everything together according to Austin's social distancing requirements. Over 200 of our chapter members worked together to provide over 200 hygiene and household supply kits for the families at Foundation Communities.*

*As we worked together in the parking lot preparing the kits, I was struck by the enormity of the need in our community. It was hard to imagine how difficult it must be for families to navigate all the challenges of coming out of homelessness, especially during a pandemic. I thought about how much stress and hurt it must cause to have to worry about providing clean diapers for one's baby.*

*At the same time, I was inspired by the generosity of our community and the willingness of people to come together to help those in need. Sammy used his position and his own time to help us achieve our goal of giving to Foundation Communities, and he inspired me by showing me how using one's position for good means everything. Our combined small act of kindness made a big difference in the lives of others, as well as in our own lives. We learned that by working together we can help our community even during a pandemic.*

# Will to Serve

In his Ultimate Gift project, Will came to understand that all it takes to serve others is the will to give of yourself and make a difference. While I'm certainly excited about the difference that the Ultimate Gift projects made throughout his high school career, I am even more excited about the impact this work will have on Will and his classmates as they make their way in the world and live a life of service. Problems are solved, and needs are met when we recognize the challenges and have the will to meet them.

## WILL SEARCY | Dallas Chapter (Texas)

*My name is Will Searcy, and I'm a senior member of YMSL Dallas. Throughout my high school years, I've had the opportunity to take a leadership role in four of our chapter's Ultimate Gift projects. In 9th grade, my mom and I worked to redesign the playground at Wesley Rankin's Community Center for the children they serve in their after-school programs, which included elementary through high school kids. We put a fresh coat of paint on all their playground equipment, planted grass, and installed basketball goals and volleyball nets. My sophomore year, during COVID, our chapter put together a sneaker drive for the St. Phillips Community Center where families would drive through, and we would hand out to all family members sneakers that had been donated by a local athletic shoe distributor. Junior year, my friends and I set up donation centers at local toy, hobby, and bookstores to secure donations for holiday gifts for teenage boys who were clients at the Dallas Children's*

Advocacy Center. We learned through that process that teenage boys are the least likely group to be bought for during holiday giving programs. Finally, my senior year, we returned to St. Phillips Community Center to put together food distribution bags for community members. The bags included all the ingredients they needed to make a healthy dinner, which we hoped would help the community learn a new way to cook for their family members.

What I learned through each of these projects was the joy in giving and the impact our group could have on the organizations we serve. I still remember watching the Wesley Rankin after-school program kids of all ages run onto their new playground with bright eyes and squeals of delight as they saw a completely transformed outdoor space. I remember hundreds of cars full of multiple-member families asking for various sizes of shoes and their big smiles when we were able to load up their trunks with brand-new high-tops. I remember my adoration for the abundant generosity of so many who came in and out of stores during the holiday season, excited to have an unknown teenage boy to shop for. I remember the heartfelt thank you we received from the St. Phillips Community Center staff as we filled over 200 food bags for their community event that would have taken them weeks to do on their own.

Over my high school years and my four Ultimate Gift projects, I learned that together, with a shared interest and plan, my group of fellow classmates and our moms were able to make an impact in a single day that would have taken the organizations we served weeks or months to have done on their own. My heart bursts with joy for being able to make that kind of impact. It's something I'll be proud of my entire life. Thank you, Jim Stovall, for inspiring our projects with your book.

# Blessings Under the Sun

Brandon describes his Ultimate Gift project, in which he helped create an open-air opportunity for people to receive food, which is the most basic of human needs. He learned a statistic that should haunt us all as he discovered that 20% of children in his community suffer from food insecurity. His powerful observation, "No human being should question when or where they will eat again," should be on all of our minds. Brandon's efforts made a difference for the people he served then and can impact us all now and into the future.

## BRANDON DUHAIME | Impact Frisco Chapter (Texas)

*Under the summer Texas sun, a row of white tables under pavilion tents lined the schoolyard. On those tables, fellow volunteers and I placed coolers of food and drinks donated by each of us. It was the Frisco Family Services Lunch Disbursement. The drive stood in place to serve local, food-insecure children a free and healthy lunch. Hunger is more common than some may understand, as 20% of Texan children suffer from food insecurity, according to the hunger-relief organization Feeding Texas. Volunteers, from grandparents to high schoolers, were each there to lend their hands to those who needed them. Soon after preparing the tables, the families began to arrive. I remember how the children raced their way over to the tables, cheerful and laughing as they took their pick of meals and snacks. We filled each and every bag we could until we ran out of meals and finished the day chatting with the families. To see the joy that our team was able to provide these families, even for a single, healthy meal, was extremely powerful.*

*With Frisco Family Services, I was able to volunteer countless more times alongside them, often in food-security-related activities such as their fruit and vegetable garden and their food bank. There was so much to learn from the lunch disbursement. No human being should question when or where they will eat again, and to meet children who suffered from such circumstances at a young age most certainly shaped my young adulthood.*

*I spent all four years of high school with YMSL, and it was within each volunteer experience that I was left with a crucial impression of the world— moments I would revisit in the years forward. From repainting walls of a preschool or packing care packages for Dallas tornado victims, each moment was understood to be crucial to the world around me. In relation to my experience with the lunch disbursement, I was reminded how essential it is to remain appreciative for all I am granted.*

*YMSL will continue to provide moments such as these to the generations that move forward within the organization, which is an absolute gift upon where they may go in the world and those they may meet along the way. These lessons cannot be taught by words but by your own hands. To volunteer your aid for others is to give the ultimate gift: to remind humanity that we exist for each other.*

# THE GIFT OF GRATITUDE

"In those times when we yearn to have more in our lives, we should dwell on the things we already have. In doing so, we'll often find that our lives are already full to overflowing."

*"I have always found it ironic that the people in this world who have the most to be thankful for are often the least thankful, and somehow the people who have virtually nothing, many times live lives full of gratitude."*

— The Ultimate Gift

# Lessons from the Library

In their Ultimate Gift project, Alex and his Young Men's Service League co-laborers created a library setting for young students who otherwise would not have access to books and other learning material. A library is more than a stockpile of books. It is a place of knowledge, inspiration, and wisdom.

As a bestselling author, I'm always embarrassed to tell people that, when I could read with my eyes as you are reading the words on this page, I don't know that I ever read a whole book cover-to-cover. After losing my sight, I discovered audiobooks through the National Library for the Blind and participated in a study to determine how fast people could listen to books and retain the lessons. Once the experiment was over, I continued with high-speed digital audio, and for the last three decades, I have literally read a book every day. Becoming a reader made me want to be a writer. But, more importantly, it opened up a whole world of possibilities to me. This is what Alex did in his community.

## ALEX BISSELL | Silicon Valley Chapter (California)

*Amidst the dusty chaos of boxes and books, mothers and their sons worked tirelessly to bring a sense of beauty and welcome to a once lifeless storeroom, now transformed into a vibrant library for students at Costaño School in East Palo Alto's Ravenswood School District. We created inspiring spaces lined with colorful beanbags, cozy nooks, and cheerful carpets for children to curl up and* read comics, novels, and poems. In the center, a gilded puppet theater crafted by YMSL members invites children to perform and watch their favorite plays.

Over several weekends, 129 members from YMSL Silicon Valley built bookshelves, sorted thousands of books, and designed the Costaño School Library as an Ultimate Gift for the Ravenswood School District. This school district is especially important to me because many of its schools are in my neighborhood. Eighty-nine percent of its students come from low-income families, and 43 percent are homeless or housing insecure. Many of the students who attend Ravenswood School District elementary and middle schools attend my high school, Menlo Atherton High School, and I think it is important that all students have access to equitable programs and opportunities no matter where they live.

After three weekends of moms and sons working together for hundreds of hours, we stood back and admired the charming and bright library filled to the brim with rainbow pigments and captivating books. I enjoyed learning how to use power tools, hang curtains, and sort library books. But more importantly, I felt grateful for the chance to make my community a more inclusive and equitable place. I came to understand the value of time, especially when focused on a cause that helps others. My chapter is proud of this Ultimate Gift, our first, that will benefit children in my community who will now have more opportunities to learn and succeed.

# The Gift that Keeps on Giving

Ryan, through his Ultimate Gift project, learned the truth and wisdom of the powerful words, "It is more blessed to give than to receive." He discovered that parents, who may have nothing of their own, don't want a gift for themselves as much as they want gifts for their children. Ryan created a memorable holiday season for families in need and created a new sense of gratitude for himself.

## RYAN KNOPF | Boulder Chapter (Colorado)

*For my chapter's Ultimate Gift project, I volunteered at Logan's Christmas Shoppe, an organization founded by Officer Logan Haymore of the Louisville, Colorado, Police Department. In 2015, Officer Haymore partnered with Ascent Community Church to provide families with an opportunity to shop for free in a pop-up style shop set up in the church where they could choose a few gifts for every child in their family.*

*I was able to volunteer on two different days and did several jobs that were needed there. These included restocking gifts on the shelves, ensuring the kids were entertained while their parents were shopping, taking families through the store and guiding them around, and, finally, wrapping gifts they had chosen. I will admit that I was not the most experienced gift wrapper, but by the end of my shift, I was looking forward to wrapping my family's gifts. I was happy to help people who could not afford gifts for their families, allowing them to choose whatever they wanted for their kids from donated items brought forth by the community. They benefited from the fact that they were able to see their kids smile on Christmas morning because of the gifts that otherwise would not have been under the tree.*

*Although Logan's Christmas Shoppe helped and benefited the families it supported, it also helped me. It made me realize that I love to help people, and being able to was such a great opportunity. My favorite part of volunteering was working with the kids while the parents shopped. The kids would tell me their life stories through the good and the bad. I remember one kid in particular whose house and all of his toys were flooded unexpectedly and ruined. Not long after, his house burned down in the Marshall fires. However, he still seemed happy, which made me realize how much his parents supported him through these tough times. It made me really happy realizing that he would have new toys under the tree on Christmas Day, and I was thankful for the opportunity to help.*

*It was genuinely surprising how much fun I had at Logan's Christmas Shoppe. I could not believe how fast the time went by while volunteering. The hours flew, and it was over before I knew it. This opportunity was undoubtedly the most fun that I have had while volunteering at YMSL. It made me realize how much I like helping people, and being able to actually meet the people I was helping made me feel great. I am looking forward to getting the chance to do it again next year.*

# Some Good Advice

All of us need to be reminded that everything we have, and the opportunity to get everything we want, was given to us through the sacrifice of veterans. Through his Ultimate Gift project, Neal learned how satisfying it can be to serve others, especially when they have given so much to serve us all. In the midst of giving to veterans, Neal received some powerful advice that will serve him well long beyond his work in the Ultimate Gift project.

## GRIFFITH NEAL ALLEN | Alpharetta Chapter (Georgia)

*Working with Veterans Empowerment Organization (VEO) for the YMSL Ultimate Gift in October 2021 was an incredibly rewarding volunteer experience. VEO is a non-profit organization that aims to provide housing, employment, and support services to homeless and at-risk veterans in the Atlanta area. As a volunteer with YMSL, I had the opportunity to work on Ultimate Gift and contribute to VEO's mission of serving veterans in need. Our group was tasked with making the outdoor space more welcoming to those who reside at the VEO campus.*

*We cleaned and pressure-washed picnic tables and benches, which we later painted. We pressure-washed and stained a very large outdoor deck. We painted a large fence and two large outdoor atriums and planted fresh flowers. We also updated a mural in the parking lot. But most importantly, we fed the resident veterans a hot meal for lunch and talked to them. I met a man who was getting ready to transition from VEO back into the community. He talked about his experience in the armed forces and how he had difficulty finding the right kind of support when he came back to the U.S. from the war in Afghanistan. He told me to listen to my mom and that it was obvious my mom cared because she was there working alongside me. He told me to never take her or my family for granted. That conversation has stuck with me for many reasons.*

*Throughout the day, I was struck by how many veterans who have served our country are in need. VEO provided our chapter with valuable insights into the challenges faced by homeless veterans, as well as the ways in which VEO works to address these issues through their various programs and services. Hearing their stories and witnessing their work firsthand was inspiring. Moreover, working alongside other volunteers from YMSL was also an enriching experience. It was heartening to see our chapter come together to support such a worthy cause.*

*Overall, my experience with Ultimate Gift and YMSL was a reminder of the importance of community service and the power of collective action. Through our efforts, we were able to make a tangible difference in the lives of veterans in need, and I left Ultimate Gift feeling grateful and fulfilled.*

# THE GIFT OF A DAY

**"Life at its essence boils down to one
day at a time. Today is the day."**

*"If we are living our lives the way we should, everything should be in such an
order that we wouldn't change the last day of our life from any other day."*

— The Ultimate Gift

# Important People

Colin discovered the vital truth that insignificant tasks become important when we perform them in service to important people, and when we get the Ultimate Gift perspective, we understand that all people are important. Until we get to know diverse people from different backgrounds, we can feel very uncomfortable and awkward. But, as Colin discovered, once we get to know people, we invariably realize that, in the important ways and where it really matters, we are all very much alike.

## COLIN JAMES WANEK | Wildcat Chapter (Texas)

*I have been a member of Young Men's Service League, Wildcat chapter, for my entire high school career and have participated in Ultimate Gift all four years. Each opportunity has been very different with unique experiences, and each one has given me a different perspective, none more so than my first Ultimate Gift when I was a fourteen-year-old freshman.*

*That year, we were working at My Possibilities, a nonprofit that offers life-skills training and socialization for adults with cognitive disabilities, or, as they call them, HIPsters (Hugely Important People). Our task was to help at the organization's new facility with some outdoor landscaping but primarily to clean. To say I wasn't excited about our shift would be an understatement, and if you've ever seen the state of my room, you know I'd rather be outside in the hot Texas sun landscaping than with a broom in my hand. It isn't easy for anyone to give up their weekend, but it can be even more difficult when you know you will be giving it up to do rigorous volunteer work.*

*Furthermore, I have to admit that the group we were serving was not one I tend to spend time around in my everyday life. The unfortunate truth is that the few times I had, I felt pretty uncomfortable around people with cognitive disabilities.*

*Our very first task was to help clean their instructional kitchen classroom. Alongside another mother and son, we got to work washing windows, wiping down countertops, and cleaning sinks. The silence while we accomplished our tasks was quickly replaced by disco music from down the hall. It turns out there was an exercise class being offered by one of the life skills coaches. Possibly out of boredom, or perhaps due to my piqued curiosity about a dead music genre, I ventured down the hall. What I saw was a group of HIPsters enjoying some dance cardio, but what caught my eye was the instructor's young son, maybe half my age, dancing alongside. When the music stopped, he didn't go seek out his dad but instead talked with the students as if they were no different than you or I.*

*This seemingly small event put a lot into perspective for me. I realized that the opportunity for these HIPsters to enjoy time together is important, that having a facility that supports their ability to thrive is vital, and that I needed to recognize how our similarities outweigh our differences. Our Ultimate Gift project, despite what seemed like menial tasks, was an important way to facilitate their success.*

*I think many of us see what a community gives us. Certainly, the ones in my life have supported me during difficult times, taught me about my faith or how to play a sport, or helped me fill my time. But as I prepare to leave these communities and move on to college out of state, I realize that it has been equally important to see how there is a direct correlation between how much I've gotten from them and how much I've devoted to them. Ultimate Gift is a way to support the communities that different nonprofits serve, but while I'll still go home to a messy room, I'll rest better knowing we helped ensure they have a (clean) place of their own.*

# Turning on the Light

During the pandemic, many serious community problems became even more critical for those among us who are less fortunate. For most of us, getting something to eat means opening the refrigerator, picking up fast food at the drive-through window, or ordering something to be delivered on a phone app. Unfortunately, in a society where food is going to waste, there are multitudes of hungry people among us. Chase discovered, through his Ultimate Gift service project, that when you deliver food along with a kind word and a bit of encouragement, you can create a feast.

## CHASE WILSON | Ozark Chapter (Arkansas)

*For our Ultimate Gift project, we worked to collect donations of packaged food and other food-related items for the Second Street Pantry during the COVID-19 pandemic. Before the pandemic, they served food to those who needed it once a week, but during the pandemic, they stopped receiving enough donations from local food organizations. This led to a large decrease in the food that the people were able to give out. My mom and I, who were already extremely active in the work of food insecurity and knew many people who needed help, decided to pitch the idea of using the Ultimate Gift to help supply food to the pantry in order to make more food bags available for those in need. After receiving the green light, we spread the word across the nearby towns and were able to collect more than enough donations for the pantry. It was shocking to see how many people, despite living through the pandemic and faced with fear, were willing to go out of their way and contribute, to the best of their ability, large quantities of food for others during the greatest time of need.*

*With the large amount of donations we received, we created food bags by the hundreds. Once all the bags were created, everyone helped to deliver them to those who needed them for the duration of a couple of weeks. Through this experience, my mom and I were able to help bring food to older people in remote communities and to others with food insecurity during the pandemic. The recipients had no one to look after them and were in need of not only food but a little conversation.*

*While I was working in my community service, I never expected to make as big of an impact on people's lives as I did. The words I write could never truly express the emotions I watched fly across the faces of those I helped. The best way to truly express it, in my mind, is the idea of turning on a light switch for someone who was stuck in darkness. That moment of impact is something unique and special that it is hard for anyone to understand without experiencing the same feeling themselves. The light that radiates from their face as they were being helped and the shine in their eyes is something that you truly never forget. The change in their world filled my drive like never before and encouraged me to give back to the community more than what was required just for the passion of it.*

*This opportunity helped to teach me about the value of having a caring community, something that I plan to not only take to college with me, but also to spread throughout the rest of my life to those around me to the best of my ability. That singular moment forever changed the way I viewed the work and world around me. What once started as another commitment that I participated in turned into a time of dedication and taught me to always lend a hand to those around me. Even without working to acquire hours or to simply move on with the organization, I stayed behind, not out of a need for hours, but rather because I felt something inside of me that wouldn't let me live with myself if I did not spend the extra time or do one last act before I left. This life-changing experience showed me that there will always be people in need and that it takes just a little bit of passion, perseverance, and courage to reach your hand out to help others. This was the true meaning, at least for me, of the Ultimate Gift, and I am forever grateful for this opportunity.*

# A Safe Place

One of the great unmet needs in many of our communities is a safe place for teenagers to congregate, relax, and spend their afternoons and evenings. Walker and his Young Men's Service League peers discovered that, in order for a place to become an oasis for teenagers, it must be clean, attractive, and fun. Their efforts transformed an obsolete space into a place where teenagers can be safe and have fun. Beyond transforming a space, they transformed the lives of the young people who will be served by the Boys and Girls Club for years to come.

## WALKER TOLPA | Fort Collins (Colorado)

*I was introduced to Ultimate Gift my sophomore year of high school. My freshman year, COVID hit, and our Ultimate Gift project didn't happen as planned. The next year, my mom ended up being the Assistant VP of Philanthropy, so I had the chance to spend a whole lot of time working on our Ultimate Gift. Our chapter decided to help renovate a Boys and Girls Club in Loveland, Colorado. Our focus of the renovation was to make the club a more inviting place for teenagers. The Boys and Girls Club told us that during the pandemic, they were worried about teenagers having a safe place to hang out. They were worried about depression and mental health with the teenagers in the community, and they wanted to entice them to come into the club to hang out with friends and do fun things together.*

*When we got there, I could see that the club really wasn't fit for teenagers. It wasn't a space where I could have ever seen myself hanging out. It was visibly geared towards a younger audience. I remember the only space they had for teenagers was a bar-style area where people could sit, make tea, and talk. I don't remember there even being many places to sit. The rest of the room was so cluttered the space was barely usable, and it certainly wasn't comfortable.*

*This is where our Young Men's Service League chapter stepped in. We were able to give the club an entire makeover. We spent one weekend in August cleaning, painting, building, creating, and innovating solutions to update and make the club look cooler. Throughout these renovations, we were able to paint the entire club; members of our chapter donated new, more comfortable furniture and TVs and brought in gaming consoles and other games for everyone to enjoy. We cleared out the clutter and cleaned it from top to bottom. By the time we were done, you couldn't even recognize the place. Most importantly, the teenagers of the community had a cooler, and overall better, space to hang out.*

*This project really helped benefit the entirety of the Boys and Girls Club. It gave the teenagers their own separate space from the younger members of the club. Once we were finished with the project, the club put on a big reveal night for all the kids. That night, our chapter got the opportunity to make crafts and host a video game tournament for the kids. The kids were so excited and grateful to have a space that felt new and usable again with fun, age-appropriate things to do. It made me so happy to hear how much the kids enjoyed their new space. I really hope that it continues to bring new members into the club. I'm so glad that the work that I did for The Boys and Girls Club was able to affect so many people in such a positive way. This project helped me see a resource in our community that I hadn't had the chance to see before. It made me realize what a benefit the Boys and Girls Club is to Loveland. I really appreciated the opportunity to help the club and the members. I was so proud of the space my peers and I were able to create for the kids.*

# THE GIFT OF LOVE

**"Love is a treasure for which we can never pay.
The only way to keep it is to give it away."**

*"...I learned that loving money leads to a hollow, empty existence. But
when you learn how to love people and use money, everything is in its proper
perspective...When we truly love others, our love makes each of us a different
person, and it makes each one we love a different person too."*

— The Ultimate Gift

# Meeting Needs and Creating Memories

Through his Ultimate Gift project, Cole discovered the value of fulfilling tangible and intangible needs for those in his community. Sometimes, people require their daily needs to be met, and other times, they need memories that will stay with them throughout their lives. Often, the greatest gift we can give anyone is to share time with them and create an impact by simply letting them know that someone cares. Cole discovered the powerful wisdom that there are no problems that cannot be faced by a committed group of people dedicated to making a difference.

## COLE WAKEFIELD | McKinney Chapter (Texas)

*Mr. Stovall,*

*Thank you for giving us YMSL Members the opportunity to share a glimpse of our eye-opening, wholesome Ultimate Gift experiences. My name is Cole Wakefield, and I'm a freshman from the McKinney (Texas) YMSL Chapter. My chapter assisted a pivotal organization in our community: Shiloh Place.*

*Shiloh Place is a shelter for single women in Collin County who have encountered financial hardship and/or domestic abuse. We were gifted with the opportunity to improve the lives of the shelter's residents through various outdoor equipment improvements.*

*We constructed a roofed structure to protect the children's riding toys from rain and other elements. The children of Shiloh Place had bikes, scooters, and* other toys to play with originally; however, they would frequently rust and become unusable as there was simply no adequate storage for them. A landscape border was also built to prevent the gravel walkway from running off during a rainstorm. YMSL McKinney also provided a working refrigerator to the shelter, allowing the mothers to purchase more than traditional food staples. For example, healthy meats can now be purchased and stored, allowing growing children to consume more nutritious and fulfilling meals. While tangible improvements to the facility continually impact the daily lives and actions of Shiloh Place's residents, our opportunity to host a carnival for them created an even greater impact, one of emotion.

After the various improvements were made to the facility, our group hosted a carnival for the mothers and their children, complete with carnival games, candy, and prizes. Seeing the joyously elated faces run out of their apartments was truly humbling and the definition of gratifying. The children had so much fun at this carnival, and I hope that it touched their hearts just as much as mine. After the carnival, the Shiloh Place Director so kindly explained that "[the] Shiloh moms [were] still buzzing about how special [we] made them feel."

I understood that we made an impact on the children by providing them with a fun experience, but the thought of creating a prolonged emotional impact on the Shiloh Place Community through such a simple gesture showed me that all it takes is an empathetic heart to create change in one's life. The word "buzzing" is what truly stuck with me as it shows that our group was able to be the match to light a fuse of happiness for families who have sadly been forced to endure much more than I could imagine.

What surprised me most about the Ultimate Gift was how much different it was from my typical individual volunteering experience. While playing bingo at a senior center, providing daycare at the Samaritan Inn, and harvesting crops at McKinney Roots are all rewarding in their own way, I feel as if the Ultimate Gift was special. Special as it created a change that was much bigger than myself. The Ultimate Gift proved to me the collective power of humanity *as I was blessed with the opportunity to see what can be created when 233 mothers and their sons work together, giving hope for those who need it most. As I continue through life, I will never underestimate the power of a group of people with a shared mission and passion.*

*Mr. Stovall, I appreciate all the work that you have done with The Ultimate Gift to showcase the impact that can be made when we choose to surround ourselves with similarly-minded people.*

# Rising from the Ashes

Whether it's in a fanciful literary story or within a seven-acre plot of land in need of regeneration, people, places, and things can find new life. Darren and his Young Men's Service League colleagues worked hard, had fun, and made a difference. Through sunshine and rain, they impacted young people in need in their community while forging memories and bonds of friendship among themselves.

## DARREN LO | Crystal Springs Chapter (California)

*Dear Mr. Stovall,*

*I am Darren Lo from the YMSL Crystal Springs Chapter's Class of 2025. Last year, our Ultimate Gift recipient was Phoenix Garden, which is a seven-acre site at San Mateo County's Youth Services Center. It is being converted from barren land to a therapeutic, regenerative oasis for at-risk youth in the juvenile center. Our project focused on Phoenix Garden's Oak Tree Nursery, where thousands of oak trees will grow from acorns in 10,000 square feet of land.*

*Our Ultimate Gift project started on a foggy October afternoon, a day after heavy rain had whipped the soil alive. Despite the historic downpour, our work area appeared surprisingly dry. My guess was a rapidly flourishing garden needed all the water it could get. When I arrived, a man in a neon reflective vest greeted us warmly, and we immediately tackled our first activity of clearing land.*

*I grabbed a rake and, with my fellow compatriots, began rooting out rocks that were lodged in the soil. Blankets of sleepy gray clouds covered the sun. However, amidst the gloominess, I heard laughter and vibrant conversation as we flattened the land.*

*The task was tiring, so we cycled through quick breaks, during which I poured myself a cup of half-and-half (meant for coffee brought by our lovely moms) and asked a mom who was on standby how Phoenix Garden got its name. Apparently, it was chosen to refer to the rebirth of land—as the area we were working on had long been desolate—but also to highlight the people the garden would support. I thought this name choice was very meaningful and representative of what we, as a volunteering organization, were hoping to achieve.*

*To me, it is heartbreaking that, despite notions of equality instilled in our society, the reality is simply not true for some children. I remember a quote from a teenager at the center, "We aren't bad kids. We're not. We just make the wrong decisions, and sometimes we need guidance in our life." Understanding I am lucky to receive an abundance of guidance, I want to give back as much as I possibly can. This garden is a medium to help, through nature, those who are less fortunate, and it is a cause I fully stand behind.*

*After about an hour, we finished our first task, and the nest for a new firebird was set. We then dispersed across the property and completed a couple other tasks. I wheelbarrowed dirt and rearranged storage areas. Hailing from a school different from most others, I initially only knew one classmate. But throughout the afternoon, I found myself, despite being a relatively reserved individual, integrated into a newfound brotherhood. We cracked jokes and shared our experiences at school and various hobbies we had in common.*

*I think there is something about nature that opens us up. As we moved into our final large task of weeding a long trail on a sloping hill, my friend from school and I were enjoying our time with people who, an hour ago, were strangers.*

*It was at this time that the clouds woke up, and it started raining again, but the quest for the Ultimate Gift never stops. We worked relentlessly through the rhythmic beating of raindrops, smiling through it all. Knowing our work was benefiting something greater than ourselves while connecting with nature kept us going strong.*

*I thought back to the metaphor of the phoenix as we continued weeding diligently. A phoenix is born from flames and ashes of its former self. A phoenix is undying, immortal, similar to our beloved Earth that nurtures all life.*

*"Young men!" At dinnertime, the end of our shift was signaled. As I locked eyes with each of the members in our weeding group, I felt an unmistakable sense of pride and joy. I realized that if the phoenix is the garden, reborn from vacant land, then my new friends and I were the flames that withstood the pelting rain, that labored to birth the phoenix and bring this amazing dream of a transformational garden to life. Even if the clouds steal the warmth of the sun, this magnificent, seven-acre phoenix will be able to offer this same warmth to not only troubled or disadvantaged youth but everybody around it. It will bring a new chapter of positivity to our community, a positivity we are all a part of and a positivity I am eager to see.*

# The Power of Perspective

As Max recounts his memories of his Young Men's Service League Ultimate Gift project several years ago, it is both powerful and poignant that the lessons he learned as a young man remain with him today as a grown man. While it's good to be impacted in the moment, it is priceless to be impacted for life. Max's memories of giving, sharing, and living out the Golden Rule shaped not only who he was but also who he is and, more importantly, who he will be in the future.

## MAX BOTHNER | Trailblazer Chapter (Texas)

*Dear Mr. Stovall,*

*I am an alumni of the YMSL Trailblazer Chapter of Fort Worth, Class of 2015.*

*My mom, Denise Bothner, was a founding member of the chapter in 2011.*

*Looking back, YMSL was one of the most valuable experiences I could have as a teenager.*

*My life as a teenager was pretty busy, balancing school work, sports, and other extracurriculars. I remember my mom gauging interest from me and friends for an organization called Young Men's Service League. We initially didn't know what to expect, just that it would be another commitment to balance. My freshman year of high school, the chapter was officially established, which included some of the local schools in Fort Worth.*

*Throughout high school, we spent time after school and on weekends volunteering at food banks, nursing homes, pet adoption facilities, the Agape Meal at Broadway Baptist Church, and picking up trash at the annual Trinity River Trash Bash.*

*I got to serve and interact with all kinds of people from my community. Not everyone had the same blessings that my friends and I had growing up, such as daily food, shelter, clean clothes, and companionship.*

*In 2011, we planned what would be our first Ultimate Gift project.*

*I was one of the team leads for the Annette G. Strauss Family Gateway Center Hallway Beautification Project in Dallas, TX.*

*We had several local YMSL chapters volunteer to clean and paint the walls of the facility. The project took two days and required some rework to clean paint that had spilled on the floor. During the first day, we were taking a lunch break outside, covered in paint. I remember a homeless man walking by and asking about what we were doing. We explained we were volunteering for the day. He asked, "What did y'all do to have to work on a Saturday?" As if we were being forced to work for punishment. We told him we were volunteers with an organization called YMSL. We had an extra lunch, and we gave it to him. I remember the look of gratitude he had, and he thanked us for our service that day. That moment taught me a lesson about helping others and having a servant's heart.*

*In today's world it is easy to focus on your own life's problems. YMSL helped me step back and see the world for what it is. Some people need help more than others. And it doesn't take much to make a difference in someone's day.*

*I am thankful for the time spent bonding with my mom, my peers, and giving back to the community through service. I encourage every young man to have a heart of service and to treat others how they would want to be treated.*

# The Ultimate Legacy Memorial Tribute

I believe it is fitting that Harrison's chapter is the last one in this book. It is a bit different as all the other chapters were written by the young men involved in their YMSL Ultimate Gift projects. But Harrison's chapter was written and submitted by his mother. When I wrote *The Ultimate Gift* book, which later became a movie, I could not have imagined what could happen when my message reached young men and their moms who were ready, willing, and able to make a difference in the world. When I wrote the sequel, *The Ultimate Life, a* book and movie, the plot involved the main character, Jason Stevens, taking the lessons he had learned in the first story and applying them in his own life. Finally, when I wrote the third installment in the trilogy, the young man, Jason Stevens, had to take the lessons he learned in *The Ultimate Gift* and applied in *The Ultimate Life* to a new level as he created *The Ultimate Legacy*.

I have long believed that we make a living based on what we receive; we create a life based on what we give; and we leave a legacy based on who we serve both now and in the future. Harrison learned lessons, gave to others, and has now created a legacy that will live on.

## AMY KRODEL | North Star Chapter (Texas)

*I am Amy Krodel, Harrison Krodel's mom. Tragically, we lost Harrison in May of 2021. I am proud and honored to contribute a memorial essay sharing the experience Harrison and I had with the Young Men's Service League and his Ultimate Gift project. I remember one time in particular when we were delivering beds to families in need for Bed Start. His reaction and how he interacted with and treated the teen boys were inspiring. It made me personally reevaluate my own preconceived notions of the recipients.*

"H," as I called him, was a special person. He was only twenty-one when he passed, but there were over 600 people at his two-and-a-half-hour-long service. It was a testament to the lives he touched in his short twenty-one years. Harrison was the most non-judgmental person I know. In his eulogy, one of his friends described how "H" liked and accepted virtually everyone. Harrison loved people, and they loved him, but he drew the line at people who treated others poorly. He was a big guy with a huge heart.

In his honor, we have started a non-profit, Hugs from Harrison, to assist teens who are aging out of foster care with housing, school, mentorship, life skills, and finding jobs. When we were deciding who would benefit from the non-profit organization, we talked about H and his life and what he would want us to do in his memory. Above all, Harrison loved his home and his family so much. He knew firsthand from his time volunteering with YMSL and through some of his friends' lives that not everyone has the blessing and support of a close family and a place to call home. He would smile knowing that Hugs from Harrison provides home and family-type support for kids in need.

# Afterword by Amy McDaniel

## YMSL Vice President of the Ultimate Gift

On behalf of Pam, Jim, and more than 25,000 YMSL young men and mothers, thank you for reading this book and joining us on our journey to bring *The Ultimate Gift* to life at the Young Men's Service League. The Ultimate Gift program embodies the spirit of philanthropy that lies at the heart of our organization. Every year, successful Ultimate Gift experiences ignite our chapters to become even more deeply connected and engaged with the communities we tirelessly serve. Like at the end of any good book, I hope your mind is racing, you are inspired, and considering what action you can take as a result.

*If you are a mom with a son, does the mission of YMSL and serving others speak to you?*

*Are you someone who thrives on making a difference in your community and is invested in developing the character of your son?*

*Does the prospect of being a leader in a chapter excite you?*

If you've answered "yes" to any of these questions and your son is currently in elementary or middle school, it's time to check whether a YMSL chapter exists in your area. If it does, determine how and when you and your son can start the membership process. However, if a local chapter does not exist, consider rallying your friends (you know the ones—the "20% of the people who do the 80% of the work" alongside you) and reaching out to YMSL National to potentially launch a new chapter. If you don't have a son but know someone who does – someone you believe would be ideal for involvement – please help us spread the word about YMSL. Our sustainability depends on finding mothers and sons who align with the goals of our organization.

Nonprofit organizations, charities, and philanthropies that see the potential in an Ultimate Gift project are invited to join us in exploring collaborative opportunities. YMSL is committed to partnering with various social service and humanitarian groups at both local and national levels each year. Are you ready to be part of a journey where collective efforts significantly lighten the load? Let's start this conversation. We're ready when you are.

Corporations, foundations, organizations, and individuals passionate about fostering leadership and service are encouraged to partner with YMSL. We aim not only to develop leadership skills among our moms and young men but also to extend a helping hand through our service work. In a world where businesses increasingly aim to leave a positive legacy, we invite you to join us. Together, we can enhance our service projects and make a meaningful difference in the lives of those we serve in our communities.

To help Jim create the book in your hands, we had more than eighty young men submit stories about the YMSL Ultimate Gift projects they completed in their communities. If you are one of those young men, know your willingness to share has far more significance than just the words on the pages of this book. Every young man who submitted a story, whether included or not, showed remarkable initiative and strength of character, representing your potential as a leader and philanthropist in the future. We are both grateful and proud of you.

Finally, if you are a current YMSL member or alumni, please allow me to express my appreciation and gratitude. Our organization finds its true essence in the incredible mothers and remarkable young men who embody our values daily. Your way of life, the decisions you take, and the profound influence you have within your community define the very core of what we stand for.

As the original text of *The Ultimate Gift* says, "In the end, a person is only known by the impact he or she has on others." Facilitating that impact in our sons, members, and communities is what YMSL is all about.

To learn more about the Young Men's Service League and the Ultimate Gift project, please contact us at:

Email: **UltimateGift@ymslnational.org**
Phone: 1-866-602-9675 (YMSL)

# About Young Men's Service League

HIS FOUR YEARS OF HIGH SCHOOL GO BY FAST,
HOW WILL YOU AND YOUR SON MAKE THE MOST OF IT?

With YMSL, you will spend quality time **together** to grow
your relationship and impact your community.

### SERVING TOGETHER
Sharing time with our son(s) while serving those in need is priceless time spent together that positively impacts our communities and strengthens our relationship with each other.

### LEARNING THROUGH EXPERIENCE
Serving philanthropies provides hands-on experiences and valuable interactions with the people we serve. Our Young Men's curriculum focuses on life skills and character development.

### BUILDING LEADERS
YMSL offers leadership opportunities for both mothers and sons through chapter jobs, teamwork, and community impact.

Learn more about the YMSL program, membership, and sponsorship opportunities, or to start a new chapter, scan here:

Learn more about becoming a recipient of an Ultimate Gift for your non-profit philanthropy or supporting a National Ultimate Gift Fund for YMSL Ultimate Gift projects nationwide

# Acknowledgments

Giving The Ultimate Gift could not exist without the incredible support and inspiration of Jim Stovall. Thank you for seeing the profound beauty in what we are doing by, as you said, "giving the Ultimate Gift: feet, hands and heart through service." It is truly an honor to represent the Ultimate Gift in this way, and working with you has been its own gift.

This Book is a reflection of the collective heart and effort of the young men and mothers of the Young Men's Service League. Their stories and growth are the essence of these pages.

Immense gratitude goes to the young men for sharing their transformative journeys and to the mothers and leaders whose wisdom and support have been invaluable.

Special thanks to Denise Bothner who first championed the Ultimate Gift as a national initiative and Amy McDaniel for her transformative impact on the program. Gratitude also goes to our National Philanthropy Team, the National Ultimate Gift Team (especially Malinda McFarlane), and the National Directors and Officers, particularly in Communications, for their enthusiasm and their invaluable contributions. Their years of phenomenal dedication and time have made YMSL what it is today.

A heartfelt shout-out to Trina Bailey, a dedicated YMSL mom, for her significant contribution to the overall design and presentation of the book. Her countless hours of work were pivotal in bringing this book to fruition.

To everyone who committed their time and passion to this project, thank you. Your involvement has not only shaped this book but also significantly enhanced our organization. The dedication and spirit demonstrated here have made us immensely proud. It's exciting to think how this will inspire more people to join us and others to lend their support to YMSL, helping us grow and make a difference across the nation.

– Pam Rosener - YMSL Founder and President

# Jim Stovall Bio

 In spite of blindness, Jim Stovall has been a National Olympic weightlifting champion, a successful investment broker, the President of the Emmy Award-winning Narrative Television Network, and a highly sought-after author and platform speaker. He is the author of more than 50 books, including the bestseller *The Ultimate Gift,* which is now a major motion picture from 20th Century Fox starring James Garner and Abigail Breslin. Eight of his other novels have also been made into movies, with two more in production.

Steve Forbes, president and CEO of *Forbes* magazine, says, "Jim Stovall is one of the most extraordinary men of our era."

For his work in making television accessible to our nation's 13 million blind and visually impaired people, The President's Committee on Equal Opportunity selected Jim Stovall as the Entrepreneur of the Year. Jim Stovall has been featured in *The Wall Street Journal, Forbes* magazine, *USA Today,* and has been seen on *Good Morning America, CNN,* and *CBS Evening News.* He was also chosen as the International Humanitarian of the Year, joining Jimmy Carter, Nancy Reagan, and Mother Teresa as recipients of this honor.

# Pam Rosener Bio

 Pam Rosener is the Founder and CEO of the Young Men's Service League (YMSL), a national non-profit organization she established in 2001. Initially founded in Plano, TX, YMSL had expanded to over 160 chapters in 22 states with close to 30,000 participants at the time of publication. Pam's leadership at YMSL involves providing vision for the organization's growth, overseeing the Board of Directors and National Leadership Team, fundraising, leadership development, and strategic planning. Under her guidance, YMSL is growing in new communities each year across America, with each new chapter contributing about 5,000 hours of service annually to their community. The organization's emphasis is on fostering mother-son relationships through impactful volunteer work. Additionally, YMSL offers a four-year curriculum for young men that enhances life skills and leadership development, with a strong emphasis on the core values of responsibility, respect, courage, perseverance, integrity, and citizenship.

Pam Rosener is also a distinguished professional and leader in the real estate industry, affiliated with The Rosener Group at Coldwell Banker Apex Realtors. Her remarkable achievements include consistently ranking in the Top 15% of all Coldwell Banker Apex Realtors and many local top producer recognitions.

## THANK YOU FOR READING THIS BOOK!

Thank you for reading this book! Here are a few free bonus resources.

### Scan the QR Code Here:

*We also would greatly appreciate your review on Amazon.com, as it helps spread the word about your enjoyment of the book and shows your support for the work of our organization. Thank you!*